THE YANKEE MINING
SQUADRON

To Captain Vanderbilt-Webb
U. S. A.

from
Lieut. W. Seward Webb, Jr.
U. S. N.
Original Officer
U.S.S. Roanoke

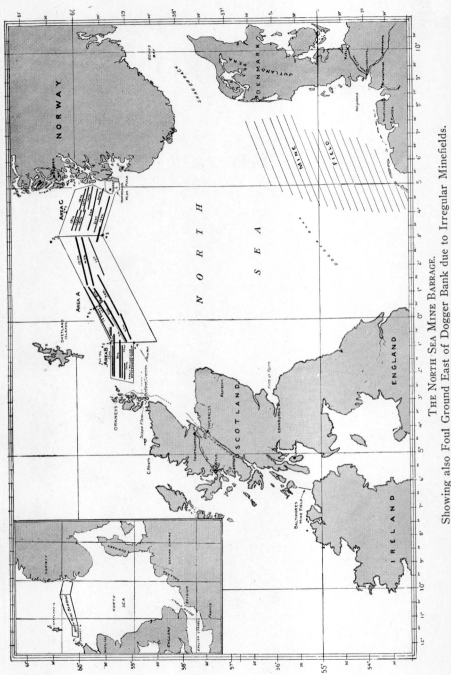

THE NORTH SEA MINE BARRAGE.

Showing also Foul Ground East of Dogger Bank due to Irregular Minefields.

The 1st to 13th Minefields were American.

THE YANKEE MINING SQUADRON

OR

LAYING THE NORTH SEA MINE BARRAGE

BY

CAPTAIN REGINALD R. BELKNAP, U. S. N.
The Squadron Commander

ANNAPOLIS, MD.
THE UNITED STATES NAVAL INSTITUTE
1920

PREFACE

In writing of the " biggest ' mine planting stunt ' in the world's history "—to quote a Christmas greeting from Rear Admiral Clinton-Baker, head of the British minelaying force—I have endeavored to make an account that would be readable enough for general interest, largely for the reason that, compared to other operations, our undertaking received scant mention at the time. Its very nature required preparation in quiet and precluded discussion of its progress. Unnecessary technical detail has therefore been suppressed, although much could be written that would be welcomed by those versed in it.

The whole account is based on data obtained at first hand. The description of assembling the squadron for a mining excursion fits the third excursion rather than the first, but the difference is a minor one, affecting only the numbers present—six ships on the first excursion, ten on the third. All the rest is correct, in substance and details.

Besides influencing an early armistice, this great minelaying operation marks an epoch in the use of submarine mines in warfare. It was an event in military history, as well as a prominent operation, and the credit for it belongs not alone to the officers and men who were actually present but also to those of the old mine force, to whose services in developing, in our navy, the art of handling and laying mines in large numbers, the success of the great operation was so largely due.

Details of the mechanical development of the new mine itself have not been gone into, for obvious reasons. Justice to that part could be done only by those who were directly concerned in it, but I am glad of the opportunity to express appreciation of the valuable service which was rendered to our cause in the war by Commander S. P. Fullinwider, U. S. N., in seizing upon and developing the long-sought means for such an undertaking, and by Lieut. Commander T. S. Wilkinson, U. S. N., and the officers and designing engineers in the Bureau of Ordnance and at the Naval Torpedo Station, Newport, R. I., by their skill and ingenuity in designing mechanical features, when normal experimenting was impossible.

As for the ships—the personal study which Captain J. D. Beuret (C. C.), U. S. N., made of the mine elevator problem was the foundation of its brilliant success, and the fact that, in the whole period of service, few alterations or improvements in the mine-layers were found desirable, although suggestions were called for, is the best tribute to those who planned and carried out their conversion.

Only very inadequate expression can be given here to my appreciation of the services of my staff, in particular Captain H. V. Butler, U. S. N., whose excellent conduct of the flagship, supported by the indefatigable care of his navigator, Lieut. Commander J. C. Cunningham, U. S. N., made it possible to approach and navigate close to unmarked minefields in the open sea. And I was fortunate to have one so thoroughly loyal and capable as Commander B. L. Canaga, without whose unremitting attentiveness, and tactful management of countless details under difficulties, our performance would have been far less creditable.

Inseparable from our recollections will always be the excellent and friendly official and personal relations with the destroyer escort, especially when H. M. S. *Vampire* led. Captain H. R. Godfrey, C. B., D. S. O., writes, " It was the determination of every officer and man in the 14th Flotilla, who had the honor of being entrusted with the screening of the U. S. Minelaying Force, that no preventable attack by enemy submarine or surface vessel should inflict damage on any ship of the Force." It is but speaking for all of us to say, that is what we felt, from the first moment of that grey morning's meeting on the day of arrival.

NEWPORT, 15 June, 1919.

CONTENTS

ILLUSTRATIONS

THE YANKEE MINING SQUADRON

CHAPTER ONE

THE MINE FORCE READY

The national anthem at morning colors woke me, and I arose and looked out. What a glorious sight! Green slopes in all freshness, radiant with broom and yellow gorse, the rocky shore mirrored in the Firth, which stretched, smooth and cool, wide away to the east and south, and in the distance snow-capped Ben Wyvis. Lying off the entrance to Munlochy Bay, we had a view along its sloping shores into the interior of Black Isle, of noted fertility. Farther out were Avoch, a whitewashed fishing village, and the ancient town of Fortrose, with its ruined 12th century cathedral. Across the Firth lay Culloden House, where Bonnie Prince Charlie slept before the battle. Substantial, but softened in outline by the morning haze, the Royal Burgh of Inverness covered the banks and heights along the Ness River, gleaming in the bright sunshine. And how peaceful everywhere! *Canandaigua* and *Sonoma* lay near by, the *Canonicus* farther out—but no movement, no signal, no beat of the engines, no throbbing pumps. All seemed resting from those last four days of our passage overseas, which had all but done away with sleep. My responsibility for the safe conduct of the squadron had ended at 1 a. m., when it dispersed at the buoy, whence the routes to our bases at Inverness and Invergordon diverged. The captains taking the ships to their berths singly, Captain Butler was up until 5 o'clock, needing daylight to take the *San Francisco* all the way in. Turned in at last, his servant and orderly at 8 o'clock were 45 minutes waking him.

The Senior British Naval officer, Captain H. F. J. Rowley, R. N., came on board early, to give us welcome, and then we went to our own chief, Rear Admiral Joseph Strauss, U. S. N., commander of the Mine Force, whose headquarters were here at Inverness, U. S. Naval Base 18. After taking a look over the base itself, Captain Murfin's work and province, we stayed to lunch at Kingsmills, a handsome place amid beautiful surround-

ings, bordering on the golf links, with gardens, tennis court, cro-
quet lawn, and fishing brook, which Admiral Strauss, Captain
Murfin, and some of the headquarters staff had rented. It was
a satisfaction to everyone to see our chief so befittingly established,
and this came out very effectively later, at a picturesque and enjoyable garden party given there on the 4th of July, an occasion
which was being celebrated locally with unaffected cordiality.
Altogether, we could feel ourselves fortunate in the beauty and
attractiveness of our surroundings and also, as we soon found,
in the hospitality and kindliness of the people.

The American Mine Force had come to Scotland, arriving May
26, 1918, to coöperate with the British in laying a great barrier of
mines, from the Orkney Islands across the North Sea to Norway.
To provide for doing our share, the small minelaying force which
our navy possessed on entering the war, consisting principally of
the old cruisers *San Francisco* and *Baltimore,* had been augmented
by eight converted merchantmen. Only six weeks before, five of
them had joined the *San Francisco,* the squadron flagship, at
Hampton Roads, Virginia, fresh from the shipyards.

The program for the newly organized squadron contemplated
the ships being in Scotland, ready for a minelaying operation, in
45 days from the time they left the shipyards. The work of
conversion having been extensive and hardly finished, the new
ships were very raw, having had but a few days to shake down.
Troubles with engines and steering gear, lost anchors, fogs, and
missing stores repeatedly interfered with training. Up to May 5,
1918, not a day had passed without a mishap or some forced altera-
tion of plan. Instead of progressing to the rehearsal of a minelaying operation by the squadron, we had been unable even to keep
all together for a single whole day. Yet we were preparing for
an operation in which, with the ships steaming close together, all
must go like clock-work, for hours without interruption.

Another week of training before going across would, therefore,
have been amply justified, but the sense of urgency was too strong.
Besides, our mine bases in Scotland needed the 500 men we were
to bring them. So, after four hustling days and nights of final
preparation, we had stolen away from Newport, Rhode Island,
just after midnight of Saturday, May 11, 1918.

Started at last! And, thanks to coöperation far and near, better
prepared than expected. There were a few quiet hours that

Sunday morning—then fog shut in thick until next day. This was trying, so early on the voyage, but as we kept together all through it, the experience only gave more confidence. Next, one ship's steering gear broke down, and she just escaped a fatal collision. The third morning, the same vessel broke down altogether. Through lucky foresight, a powerful tug, *Sonoma,* was with us, which towed the disabled ship 150 miles until next morning, when the break was repaired.

The submarines that soon afterwards appeared on our coast were known to be crossing the Atlantic now, so we had target practice next afternoon, to be ready for them. Then I felt we could give a good account of any surface attack. Torpedoes, fire, and collision were what we had to fear. All the ships had mines on board and, since we steamed only 500 yards apart, an explosion in one ship would have involved the others.

Crossing in our company was the big collier *Jason,* loaded with an aviation station outfit for Killingholme, England, which afterwards did good work. On the tenth day, heavy weather came on, and *Jason* disappeared in a black squall, rolling heavily and steering far off the course. She being a sister of the ill-fated *Cyclops,* and no trace of her showing in four days, added considerably to the anxiety felt as we entered the active submarine zone. Radio calls brought no response. We had all but given her up, when, at early daylight, just before the appointed rendezvous with the destroyers, she came lumbering up astern. And so, notwithstanding the many vicissitudes in 3000 miles steaming, we met the escort with our number complete and right on the dot, in time and place.

Our arrival off Inverness the following midnight, May 25-26, 1918, made the Mine Force complete as to constituent parts necessary for the operation in hand. The *Baltimore* and *Roanoke* had preceded the others, making us seven. Three more were still in shipyard hands, but there was no need to wait for them before beginning the minelaying.

Between operations the squadron was divided for loading, half at Inverness (Base 18), and half at Invergordon (Base 17), 30 miles away. Being intended for the storage and assembly of mines—all that we used came from America—these bases had scant means at first for assisting the ships. Their needs could be supplied from the Royal Naval Dockyard and two depots, under Rear Admiral E. R. Pears, R. N., and Captain Tancred at Invergordon, and Captain Rowley at Inverness, who were always cordially responsive to our requests.

The motto for all American naval forces abroad, however, was to be self-supporting, and thanks to our provident first supply and to regular replenishment by the mine carriers, we had to draw on the British stocks for very little. After a month, the repair ship *Black Hawk* arrived. She took no part in minelaying, being always moored off Inverness, separate from the Mine Squadron and flying Rear Admiral Strauss' flag, but her equipment of machine tools and repair material made the Mine Force normally independent in regard to upkeep. Except for docking, we asked very little of the British in the way of repairs.

Upon one occasion, the soluble salt washers for the principal safety device of the mines nearly ran out, the local atmospheric conditions having caused many more to be used than estimated. No washers of the right size and kind were obtainable anywhere inside three weeks, and thus a shortage of these atoms—the size of a peppermint " Life Saver "—threatened to hold up the laying of 5000 mines. The *Black Hawk* had a steam press, however, and could make a die—and by the time they were needed, washers in plenty were ready—incidentally of better quality than before.

While the ships were unloading the mines they had brought, for overhaul on shore, and were coaling and otherwise preparing for minelaying, the larger preliminaries were taken up at a conference of Rear Admiral Strauss and myself with Admiral Sir David Beatty, Commander-in-Chief of H. B. M. Grand Fleet. Vice Admiral Brock, his Chief of Staff, Rear Admiral Clinton-Baker, the British Rear Admiral of Mines, Captain Lockhart-Leith, the head of his Staff, and Captain R. A. Pound, of the Admiralty, attended this conference, which was held on board the flagship *Queen Elizabeth,* at Rosyth, Thursday, 30 May, 1918.

First came the subject of tactics, and I explained my plan, to lay the mines with the squadron steaming in line abreast, ships 500 yards apart, making a trace on the chart like a music score. Three vessels (later five) would be laying mines simultaneously. When a ship had emptied herself of mines, her neighbor, ready and waiting while steaming alongside, would begin. At the end of the minefield, some temporary small buoys would be planted, by which to pick the field up later, to continue it. This plan was accepted without comment.

The area to be mined having been publicly notified two months before, the enemy might have placed some mines there, on the random chance of damaging our force. The only arrangement practicable to meet such a contingency was for some of the destroyer escort to explore for mines ahead of the minelaying formation as it proceeded. Only those ships would be fully protected that might be following directly in the wake of the searching destroyers, the main purpose being to discover the existence of an enemy minefield in time for the squadron to maneuver aside.

A clear understanding was reached at the conference of the relation of the mine squadron and its escort to the supporting force. The mine squadron being lightly armed and of moderate speed, it would have been at great disadvantage against even a numerically weaker force of light cruisers, with their superior batteries and speed. Hence the need of the support, which would consist of a battleship or battle cruiser squadron, or both, and of light cruisers, according to the estimated risk of attack at the time. If attack threatened, the mine squadron and its destroyer escort would seek safety in the direction ordered by the Support Commander; otherwise they would proceed on their mission and return to base afterwards, according to the program for that occasion. The destroyer escort would be of strength sufficient to ward off any probable attack by submarines or by surface vessels that might elude the supporting force and the regular patrols.

The location of the first minefield was decided upon; then further details were settled with Vice Admiral Brock and Rear Admiral Clinton-Baker, for the first mining excursion, which was to be done by the American and British squadrons at the same time. Preparatory notice was to be given by the Commander Mine Force to the Admiral of the Grand Fleet at least four days before the time the mine squadron was expected to be loaded and ready for an excursion. Upon a second, definite notice, not less than 48 hours in advance, when it was certain that the squadron would be ready, a combined operation order would be issued by the Admiral, naming all the forces concerned and containing the instructions and intelligence necessary for all.

2

After lunching on board with Admiral Beatty, Rear Admiral Strauss and I took our leave. We had a look at Holyrood Palace and a walk through Canongate Street that afternoon, returning to Inverness next day. Not enough material had yet been accumulated to assemble mines to fill all seven minelayers present, but 3400 would be ready in a few days, sufficient to lay a field 47 miles long, consisting of one row of mines at each of the three levels prescribed. A mine embarking schedule was made out accordingly, to include *San Francisco, Baltimore, Roanoke, Canandaigua, Canonicus,* and *Housatonic,* for a start on June 7.

CHAPTER TWO

THE NEED AND THE MEANS

A barrier of high explosive across the North Sea—10,000 tons of TNT, 150 shiploads of it, spread over an area 230 miles long by 25 miles wide and reaching from near the surface to 240 feet below—70,000 anchored mines each containing 300 pounds of explosive, sensitive to a touch, barring the passage of German submarines between the Orkneys and Norway—this was the final five months' contribution of the American and British mining forces towards bringing the war to a close.

To stop the enemy submarines near their bases, before they could scatter on the trade routes, would obviously defeat their campaign more surely than merely hunting them at large. That was the purpose of the Northern Mine Barrage, which, with the barrage at Dover, made it not impossible but extremely hazardous to enter or leave the North Sea. That many a submarine came to grief in attempting these barriers is now a certainty, and the establishment of the Northern Barrage, which many had thought impossible, insured the early finish of the submarine campaign.

The resumption of ruthless submarine warfare became a serious threat to the cause of the Allies, and at the time of our entry into the war their situation was critical—how much more critical than the world was allowed to know at the time, Admiral Sims has disclosed in his " The Victory at Sea." The relief brought about through the convoy system, in which our destroyers, the navy's first participants, had a large share, was immediate and important. But the submarine menace was far from ended and—according to the best information—would soon be greatly augmented, while the increasing number of transports would offer the enemy more opportunities, with the added horror of troopship sinkings in prospect.

Of further measures, the most effective would be such a blockade as would keep the submarines in or from their bases. The British had already mined a large area north and west from Heligoland, but this obstruction was not insurmountable, for the

Germans from nearby could always clear a passage through when wanted. In any case, until the Skagerrack passage were closed, the submarines might use that route without hindrance. Two weighty reasons kept the Skagerrack open—unwillingness to violate neutral waters, and the ease with which German forces could raid any barrier near their bases. It may be recalled with what sudden damage a small German cruiser detachment raided a convoy just outside the Skagerrack, in October, 1917.

To be effective, therefore, any barrier must be beyond easy reach of a raiding force and cover the Skagerrack, and must also be far enough to the northward of the British bases not to hamper the battle fleet's engaging with the enemy. Hence, the anti-submarine barriers should be, one near Dover Strait, the other across the North Sea, from Scotland to Norway.

The closing of Dover Strait, undertaken by the British Navy alone, needs no further mention here. Although the strong tidal currents there, frequent rough seas, and hard, smooth bottom were unfavorable for minefields, other means—such as a line of guard vessels moored not far apart and equipped with powerful searchlights, together with numerous active patrollers—were employed with a considerable degree of success.

The Northern Barrage would be too long a front, and much of it too far from base, for effective patrol without a great number of vessels. A wide, thickly sown minefield, however, would watch night and day in all weathers without relief, and would be even more effective against passage submerged than against passage on the surface, because of the less wear and disturbance of the mines by wave action, deep down under water.

Currents were not strong in the northern location, but the bottom lay as deep as 900 feet, whereas 300 feet had heretofore been the deepest water ever mined. Merely to provide the mines meant a large undertaking, besides involving an enormous quantity of the same high explosive which was likewise in heavy demand for shells and bombs. Supposing the mines ready, the planting of so many would be a long and dangerous operation, employing all the Allies' existing minelayers indefinitely. And neither the British nor ourselves yet had a mine that was quite satisfactory for the prospective requirements.

Our Naval Bureau of Ordnance, however, was intent on finding the means for such a barrier, so that when, in May, 1917, among the many contrivances offered for winning the war, Mr. Ralph E. Browne, an electrical engineer of Salem, Massachusetts, presented his submarine gun for consideration, Commander S. P. Fullinwider, U. S. N., in charge of the Bureau's mining affairs, saw that, although the invention was not suitable for naval purposes in the form offered, a new electrical device which it contained, if applied to the firing mechanism of a submarine mine, would result in just what we were looking for—a mine at once sensitive and far reaching. Mr. Browne collaborated with the Bureau of Ordnance in developing the new mine-firing device. By July, 1917, all doubt as to its practicability had been dispelled and the Bureau of Ordnance was able to give assurance that, in urging the closing of the German bases, our navy might offer the means.

Extravagant claims were common in the field of mining inventions, and three years of war lessons in the perversity of mines made the British naturally skeptical of this American find. An experienced officer in mining was sent over to see, Lieutenant R. H. DeSalis, R. N., who had received the D. S. O. for some minelaying on the Belgian coast. As the new device was put through its paces before him, the chill thawed out and in two hours he had become almost an enthusiast. Upon his report the British Admiralty took up the plan with active interest.

Upon returning from London in mid-October, 1917, Admiral Mayo, of our Atlantic Fleet, brought back the outline of a proposed minelaying operation. The paper was quite informal—unsigned, undated, bearing in pencil across the top, " Admiralty would be glad to learn whether Navy Department concur in the plans as shewn."

The field was to be 230 miles long—the distance from Washington to New York—divided into three parts, the middle section, of 135 miles, called Area A, allotted to us, because the reach of the new American mines was greater than ordinary—three of them covering the same extent as eight mines of other types. Thus numbers and effort were saved.

There would be three " systems," each consisting of one or more rows of mines just below the surface, dangerous to any craft, and other rows at intermediate and extreme depths, so that, whether running on the surface or at ordinary submergence or as deep as 240 feet, a submarine had the odds against her. In the absence of patrol vessels to drive them down, submarines would naturally run on the surface, and so the rows of upper level mines were made more numerous than those at deeper levels. The stroke of a mine is sudden and powerful, and while a vessel on the surface may survive it, to a submerged submarine it is usually fatal. All classes of vessels shy at a minefield, and that the Germans shared this aversion was shown by captured papers, which made it clear that the submarines dreaded nothing so much as mines.

The scheme was unprecedented, and that its great magnitude would involve a mass of detail requiring very careful adjustment was evident on the most cursory examination. Some who heard of it regarded it as impossible, and foolish to attempt. As to the new mines, the very basis of the whole project—since a complete unit would not exist for several months, the statement of Rear Admiral Ralph Earle, Chief of the Naval Bureau of Ordnance, that the mines would be forthcoming in season, had to be based upon tests of the mine only by parts, with the assumption that all would function properly when assembled. Action upon that assurance would at once involve upward of forty million dollars, which made his stand a bold one, inviting unmeasured odium, should the mine after all fail. To await the mine's final proving, however, would have been fatal to any possibility of beginning the barrage before 1919.

The task of laying the barrier would be hazardous in itself, with constant danger of interruption by the enemy. A single minefield in the open sea, or widely separated ones, presented no extreme difficulties, but to lay a series of them so close together as to leave no considerable gaps between, made a problem for which no really practical solution was yet visible.

For four days the project was under consideration by the Naval General Board at Washington. Time pressed, the need was great, the new mine very promising. The attitude of our officers was favorable. My own expressed view, based on three years' experience in mining, was that, though much greater difficulties and magnitude would develop even than yet foreseen, the scheme was nevertheless feasible, was within our minelaying experience in principle, and, though it could hardly be more than half or a quarter effective, it was well worth doing. The British Admiralty's approval and belief in the practicability of the scheme was implied in the original paper, but an explicit confirmation was asked and obtained by cable, on the basis of their three years' war experience and knowledge of North Sea conditions. And so the plan went to the Secretary of the Navy bearing the General Board's approval, as promising a sufficient degree of success to warrant undertaking it.

CHAPTER THREE

The Bases in Scotland

The British Minelaying Squadron was to operate from Grangemouth, near Rosyth, on the Firth of Forth. As a mine assembling and operating base for the American Squadron, the British naval authorities decided on Inverness and Invergordon, in the Scottish Highlands, situated on Inverness Firth and Cromarty Firth, re-

MINE ASSEMBLY AND STORAGE SHEDS.
U. S. Naval Base 18, Inverness.

spectively, which empty into Moray Firth about eight miles apart. One base would have been enough and in some respects more convenient, but the limited transportation means across Scotland necessitated two. To require the slow mine carriers to navigate the difficult passages around the north of Scotland would prolong their exposure to submarines and cause more escort duty for destroyers, so it was decided to discharge their cargoes on the west side, at points which gave a short haul across Scotland—Fort William, at the western terminus of the Caledonian Canal, and Kyle of Loch Alsh, where one crosses to the Isle of Skye. The cargoes were transported by canal motor-barge and by the Highland Railway.

In order to issue mines to the ships ready in all respects for planting, the bases needed a large number of men for shop work, besides others for transportation, police, clerical work, messmen, and sanitation. The entire establishment on shore was under Captain O. G. Murfin, U. S. N., who had 20 American naval officers and 1000 enlisted men at each base, 3 officers and 60 men at each of the unloading points, Fort William (actually at Corpach village) and Kyle. Headquarters was at Inverness, because of its superior communications and more central location. Captain Murfin had sailed November 13, for England, to supervise the preparation of the bases. With him had gone Commander T. L. Johnson, then commanding the small minelayer *Dubuque,* who was to inform himself fully on the situation and return to Washington as soon as practicable with answers to a long list of questions—everything we could then think of as useful to know for intelligent coöperation in the preparations.

The large, substantial, stone buildings of two idle distilleries, Dalmore, three miles out from Invergordon, and Glen Albyn, at Muirtown, where the Caledonian Canal locks out to Inverness Firth—clean, dry, and well ventilated—gave excellent living accommodations for the men. The smaller buildings made suitable offices, but considerable additions were made for messing, cooking, and washing arrangements. A Y. M. C. A. hut was established in each base, and at Inverness the little Muirtown Hotel was transformed into a small hospital. This, and similar provision at Dalmore, all under Captain E. J. Grow (M. C.), were for mild or emergency cases. The main dependence for hospital care was Strathpeffer—a " hydro " cure in peace time—20 miles from either base. There a U. S. Naval Base Hospital of 1000 beds had been established, under Captain E. S. Bogert, Medical Corps, with the Leland Stanford unit.

The buildings for mine assembly and storage were erected on adjacent vacant land, spur tracks being brought in from the main railway line, thus making good communication between the two bases, as well as with their receiving sources and shipping out points. Most of the machine tools and other shop and office equipment, as well as furnishings for the men's use, came from the United States.

Some dredging was done in Inverness Firth to admit our minelayers into Beauly Basin, near the canal entrance. The navigation marks for entering the Firth were improved, because ordinarily vessels of our size seldom came in there, and then only by day. In addition, the whole length of the Caledonian Canal was lighted, for night navigation by the mine carrying lighters.

Labor was scarce in the Highlands and the weather that winter was severe. The work went slowly, delayed considerably beyond expectation. Captain Murfin had many discouragements, and disappointments in deliveries from the United States. In spite of the kindness of all about him, he must often have felt very far away from home; but afterwards, the frank admiration repeatedly expressed by all visitors to the bases must have repaid his six long months of effort. In the end, the bases were ready in time, and their capacity, and the rate of transportation as well, were twice the original estimate, the two bases together being capable of assembling 1000 mines a day ready for planting.

Sending over the base personnel began with small drafts in December, but as accommodations for the full number were not ready soon enough, and the demand to use all transportation for troops became pressing during the Germans' great drive in March, 1918, the base complements were not more than about two-thirds full when the mine squadron sailed from the United States coast in May. The greater part, 750, of the number then lacking had therefore to be brought over by the squadron. Though this retarded the proper organizing of the base personnel, it did not delay the minelaying.

CHAPTER FOUR

The Supply of Mines

In the same past six months other preparations, too, had been pushing ahead, both at home and abroad.   Providing the mines—

A Mine in Mid-Air, Being Hoisted in.
The Plummet is at the Lower Left Corner.

the task of our Naval Bureau of Ordnance—would alone make a story of great interest.   Considering how long it had taken to develop previous types of mines, to have made a success of an invention that was new since our entering the war was indeed remarkable, the more so from inability to test a single mine complete before ordering 100,000.

Mines for the open sea in great numbers, moored " flying "— that is, by ships steaming at considerable speed—need anchors with automatic depth regulation. Such mechanism had undergone important changes during the war, and the new American mines

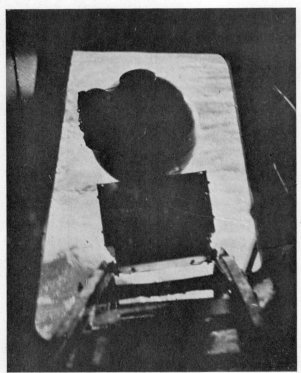

LAUNCHING A MINE THROUGH THE STERN PORT.
There is a Nine-Foot Drop, from Rails to Water.

needed all the improvements, to make them sure to plant at the intended level. They were to be much deeper than ever attempted before, and also in deeper water.

Three British officers of considerable mine experience assisted here, Lieut. Commander H. O. Mock, R. N. R., Lieutenant R. H. DeSalis, R. N., and Lieut. Commander Harold Isherwood, R. N. V. R. The last was an expert designer, and had an important part in planning our new mine anchor, which was similar to a late model British mine anchor.

A submarine mine of to-day consists of a mine case, shaped like a ball or egg, about one yard in diameter, mounted on an anchor in the form of an iron box about 30 inches square, connected by a wire rope mooring cable, about ⅜ inch in diameter. The mine case contains the charge of high explosive—300 pounds of TNT in our mines—and the firing mechanism. The combination stands about 5 feet high and weighs 1400 pounds. Four

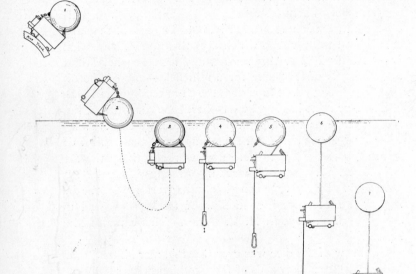

THE SEQUENCE OF OPERATIONS AFTER A MINE IS LAUNCHED.

small car wheels on the anchor run on steel tracks, allowing the mines to be easily moved along the decks to the launching point.

When the mine dives overboard, the mine and anchor come to the surface and float for a time, still held together, part of the mine case above water. Outside the anchor is a 90-pound plummet, containing a reel of ⅛-inch diameter steel wire " plummet cord," made the same length that the mine is to be below the surface. Thus, if the mine is to be 160 feet beneath the surface, the cord is made 160 feet long. The plummet drops off when the mine goes overboard, unreels its cord, coming to the end with a jerk that trips the slip hook which holds the mine and anchor together. The pull on the cord also lifts the latch on the reel inside the anchor, allowing the mooring wire to unwind. The nearly solid plummet tends to sink faster than the more bulky anchor, thus keeping the cord taut until the plummet strikes bottom. The cord then at once slackens, releasing the latch, locking the reel, and preventing any more mooring wire unwinding. The anchor, continuing to sink, pulls the mine under until the anchor strikes bottom. The mine is thus finally moored always at the desired depth beneath the surface, no matter how irregular the ocean bed may be. The mine cases are buoyant enough to pull straight up from their anchors ordinarily, but in a current they are swayed away from the vertical, which dips them down somewhat deeper than intended. For this reason, any locality where the currents are strong is unfavorable for a minefield—one of the difficulties the British Navy had to contend with in closing the Dover Strait.

The new mine having, by October, been carried past the experimental stage as to its principal features, by the Naval Torpedo Station at Newport, R. I., some important mechanical details of the mine yet remaining were now worked out by the *Baltimore,* Captain A. W. Marshall, working directly under the Bureau of Ordnance. By the time complete units were ready, the *Baltimore* had been sent abroad, so the proof testing devolved upon the *San Francisco,* Captain H. V. Butler. This came in March and April.

No throw of the dice was ever watched more intently than those first proof tests. Upwards of forty million dollars had been staked on them and were already half spent. Results on the first day made us feel easy, but it was two days more—from various delays—before we succeeded in exploding a full loaded mine. This had been planted in Chesapeake Bay, well marked and guarded, in the very same deep hole where a whirlpool effect troubled the German submarine *Deutschland* on her first return trip. It was not possible to place the mine far from the fairway, however, since the water elsewhere was not deep enough for our purpose. Early the second morning, the battleship *Arizona* came along, heading too near it. The signal " You are standing into a minefield! " sent her rudder hard over and engines full speed astern. We could see the mud stirred up, from two miles away. Since we could not get the mine up, what a relief it was when it was set off at last by sweeping!

The final proving of the mine as a whole, which was completed in April, off Cape Ann, did not take place until after several cargoes of mine parts had been shipped abroad, but the mine's success, from its first trials, showed how careful and observant had been all those who were concerned in its designing and testing.

The prospect in October was that the shipment of mines would begin in January, but through delay in completing the detailed plans and from the abnormal industrial conditions prevailing, these shipments did not attain a regular flow until May, so that the ships and the mines were ready together.

Secrecy, as well as timely delivery, caused the manufacturing to be partitioned among 500 contractors and sub-contractors, some of them as far west as the Mississippi. Certain mine parts from different makers were put together by still others, and all parts flowed toward Norfolk, Virginia, the trans-Atlantic shipping point. Planning this dividing up, placing the contracts, and arranging for the inspection of all—taking into account the transportation involved and the many different kinds of firms—wire rope makers, automobile concerns, foundries, machine shops, electricians, die-presses, and even candymakers—it was indeed a complex web. What tireless industry and what endless patience under pressure went into this work, only Commander Fullinwider and his assistants can fully appreciate.

A large plant to charge the mines with explosive was built alongside the Naval Magazine at St. Julien's Creek, near the Norfolk Navy Yard. This plant was of capacity larger than any other of the kind, ample for handling 1000 mines a day. The high explosive was melted in steam kettles to about the consistency of hasty pudding, and drawn off, 300 pounds of TNT at a time, into the mine spheres. An automatic device shut the flow off at the right weight, and a mechanical conveyer carried the mines along slowly, to the pier end, by which time they would be cool enough to load into the waiting ship. Hot work around those steam kettles through the long summer! A quiet but important corner, handling 25,000,000 pounds of TNT, with constant risk from fire. Several of the sailors were overcome by the kettles' poisonous fumes, and one died. The duty was monotonous and inconspicuous but was done with praiseworthy faithfulness.

CHAPTER FIVE

GENERAL SUPPLIES AND TRANSPORTATION

Under the extraordinary demand prevailing abroad for food and all kinds of military material, it was only fitting that ordinary supplies for our part of the Northern Barrage operation should come from America, British sources to be used only for fuel and fresh provisions. Details are needless here, except to mention their completeness—largely due to the efforts of Captain G. C.

A MINE CARRIER STEAMER.
Twenty-Four of These were Constantly Employed to Transport the Mine Parts Over to Scotland for Assembly and Laying.

Schafer of the Pay Corps. After starting things fair at home, he sailed about mid-December for England, where the needs of the bases could be best determined. With him went Assistant Paymaster R. N. Smither, U. S. N. R. F., who later became his successor, and Lieutenant Thomas Newhall, U. S. N. R. F., who had been enrolled for duty principally in connection with transporting the mine carriers' cargoes across Scotland. His experience in railroading and his tactful energy made a valuable asset. After their departure, purchases and deliveries were followed up indefatigably by Assistant Paymaster A. B. Peacock, U. S. N. R. F., who was quite successful in bringing pressure to bear effectively. One morning, after a certain freight car had been missing for two weeks, he reported that eight railroad presidents were now interested personally in the search—and the car was then found.

For transportation beyond the seaboard, cargoes of mines must go in special ships, which could carry also the general supplies for the operation. The mine carriers should be small rather than large, to minimize the effect on the progress of the operation in the event of losing one. About 60,000 tons in constant employment being needed, 24 of the so-called "Lake" steamers were selected, built on the Great Lakes for coastwise service, of 2500 tons average capacity. They were armed against submarines, manned by naval crews, and would sail in convoy, two or three every eight days, beginning in February. Their fitting out and management came under the Naval Overseas Transport Service, which furnished them according to schedule. Slow speed, due to their small size and cheap build, made them good prey for submarines, which sank one of these carriers in April, the *Lake Moor,* with 41 of her crew—almost our only loss of life in the whole operation. This was another part of the whole operation that was obscure, though all-important, which would yet have been very conspicuous had it not been so well done.

The great amount and the dangerous nature of these cargoes needed special arrangements for embarking them, for which Southern Railway Pier No. 4, at Pinner's Point, opposite Norfolk, Virginia, was taken exclusively. This pier being large enough to assemble several cargoes at once, the entire cargoes could be loaded there, and that was the plan, until the great disaster at Halifax aroused strong local opposition concerning the place of loading the mines on board. It was too late then to relocate the plant for charging the mines with TNT, and as the ground of local opposition was undeniably well taken, a real problem was presented. To take the loaded mines in lighters from the magazine 17 miles to the Explosives Anchorage, as first proposed, would have been very slow—almost impossible in bad weather—even had ample towage, lighterage, and labor been available, besides involving an extra handling for every mine, with attendant damage and risk. Thanks to the timely exertions of Captain W. J. Maxwell, U. S. N., who was in general charge of the loading and despatch of mines, a channel was dredged up to the magazine pier, where the steamers could embark the mines directly, after loading

3

the unobjectionable part of their cargoes at Pier 4. Thus local interests were quieted with the greatest measure of safety.

Several ingenious arrangements were devised for handling the mine material quickly. Two mine anchors fastened together, 1600 pounds, could be trundled about by one man, making a considerable labor saving on loading 2000 in one cargo. The pier became also the sub-assembly point for some mine parts, requiring a shop, as well as shipping organization. All was done by naval enlisted men, under the supervision of Lieutenant A. J. Love and Lieut. Commander R. E. Corcoran (P. C.). It was not long before these steamers began to take supplies also for our Battle Squadron with the Grand Fleet, 500 tons at a time.

CHAPTER SIX
A Sample of Quality

While details were shaping for proving the mine early in March, an urgent request came from the British Admiralty for one or more minelayers to help lay a field in the North Irish Channel. This passage was used by slow convoys to the west coast, making port first at Lamlash in the island of Arran, and submarine activity here needed to be checked. The sinking of the *Tuscania* had taken place in this vicinity.

At that time, only the *San Francisco* and *Baltimore* could be considered for this duty, and as the former was flagship, the *Baltimore* was sent. To " How soon can you go? " over long distance wire, Captain Marshall answered " Right away," guessing at the destination, and on March 4 he sailed from New York to join H. M. S. *Leviathan* as escort for a fast convoy out of Halifax.

By popular standards, the *Baltimore* was a musty back number—years older than many of her officers and crew—but she had been at Manila Bay with Dewey and had otherwise distinguished herself in a long and varied career. Though classed as a poor steamer, the ease with which, time after time, she produced extra speed at a pinch was a standing joke. Thanks to a good overhaul early in the war and to the ability and contagious enthusiasm of her engineer, Lieutenant R. P. Molten, U. S. N., she now topped a 9-day transatlantic run at 13 knots, for the most part in rough weather, with a three-hour spurt at 18.6 knots—2 knots faster than was supposed to be safe for her engines—just to keep pace with the *Leviathan*.

She arrived at Greenock, Scotland, March 17, ready for work, but was so much earlier than expected that her first mines were not delivered until April 13. Without any preparatory trials, though the mines were British, of a type new to the *Baltimore,* she went out at once, beginning the deep minefield between the island of Islay and the Irish coast, which was to prevent submerged but not surface passage.

More mines in excess of her reported capacity having been sent to her, 10 had to be carried on the upper deck, and the last one of these mines, in going down the elevator, was jambed, due to the roll of the ship, and held suspended in the elevator shaft. William J. Powers, gunner's mate, 1st class, promptly of his own initiative, at imminent risk of the 1800-pound weight falling or one of the mine's firing horns breaking, removed the detonator and with it the great menace to the ship. Before the *Baltimore's* next trip, her own mechanics extended the launching deck tracks, to accommodate 180 instead of 170 mines, since the British naval authorities wished her to plant the larger number each time. Four times more she planted 180 mines, April 18, 21, 28 and May 2, planting always at night, in an area infested with submarines.

Extra careful navigation was required, both to lay the mines just where intended, as their anchor cables had been cut to fit (anchors not automatic), and to approach close to the mine-fields previously laid, yet avoid them. In one such operation, the gyro-compass went wrong at a critical moment. The navigator, Lieut. Commander George W. Hewlett, U. S. N., kept his head and held his peace, applying the corrections to the magnetic compass with coolness and accuracy, as if maneuvering to avoid a sand bank, instead of to clear a minefield by only 500 yards.

The *Baltimore* laid this whole minefield unassisted, 899 mines in all. She worked directly under Rear Admiral Clinton-Baker, R. N., who wired his congratulations upon the successful completion of the first three operations, and when, at the end of May, she was recalled to our squadron, he wrote to Captain Marshall:

Once more I wish to thank you for all that you have done and for the very willing help which you, your officers and ship's company have always given. It is much to be regretted that the work which you commenced and so admirably carried out is not to be completed, at any rate for the present, though doubtless you will be doing equally useful work elsewhere in the near future. Good luck to you and your ship.

This minefield accounted for two enemy submarines and there was little further submarine activity in that vicinity, which should be credited largely as an achievement of our squadron. And as a sample of quality before the North Sea mining began, the *Baltimore's* work gave our colleagues confidence that we could do our part—by far the largest portion—in that great, open sea operation. As immortalized in our song:

> "The *Baltimore* was the first away.
> She traveled a thousand miles a day,
> To show the Allies the lively way
> Of the Yankee Mining Squadron."

CHAPTER SEVEN
MINE ASSEMBLING AND EMBARKING

Following the conference on board the *Queen Elizabeth,* our bases worked full blast on the mines for the first operation. One group assembled and tested the anchors, another the mines, a third the plummet, a fourth the plummet and anchor together, and a fifth, the final assembly, of mine and anchor complete—called a unit. A section of mine track of standard gauge sufficed to test the anchor wheels and thus obviate trouble on board from their binding or dropping between the ship's tracks during mine-

MINES AND MINE ANCHORS AWAITING ASSEMBLY.
The Anchors were Shipped in Pairs, for Convenience in Handling.

laying, possibly causing an interrupted string. It speaks well for the manufacture, for the testing at the bases, and for the ship's mine track installations, that no such interruption ever occurred in the whole series of operations.

The adjustment of firing mechanism was done in a locked room, the secret entrusted only to a few. It was delicate work, to be done patiently and methodically, for its accuracy determined whether the mine would be alive—or a dud. Fidelity in such adjustments is hard enough to maintain when the repetitions are numbered only by tens. Where hundreds and thousands are involved the tax on attention becomes severe.

Before loading the mines into the cars, for transfer to the lighters, each mine was primed with a mealed TNT " booster " charge and the firing detonator was put in place—all ready for the

laying—and five safety devices were seen in place and in order.
These devices would prevent the firing mechanism working until
the mine had reached a certain minimum depth under water and
had been in the water about 20 minutes, and would also prevent
exploding in case of loss overboard during embarking. Such
devices usually function properly, and dependence is not placed
on one alone but on several together, any one of which will make
the mine safe to handle—by experienced men. At an early stage
in the training in mines, one learns to treat them with respect
always—no liberties. Even the safest explosives, the surest mechanism, have an occasional, inexplicable aberration.

LOADING MINES INTO LIGHTERS.
At Base 18, on the Caledonian Canal, at Inverness.

The ready mines are swung up into open freight cars, for hauling to the water side, whence they go, 40 to 80 together, in lighters
out to the ships. After being landed on the tracks of the minelayer, one safety pin is removed—leaving four—and the mine is
then examined for any derangement during the three handlings
in transit from the store shed.

The north of Scotland was a barred area, yet it was reported possible for information to get through to the enemy in 18 to 20
hours—time enough for interference to hatch out. With so much
activity at the bases, lighters going to the ships loaded and returning empty, and a large destroyer escort coming in on 5 June, the

fact that an operation was in early prospect was obvious. The *hour* of departure at least could be kept secret, and the start was fixed for midnight. The two detachments of the mine squadron and the destroyer escort would assemble at 1 o'clock a. m., 7 June, just outside the Sutors, the high rocky headlands at the mouth of Cromarty Firth. On this first occasion the preparations continued until one hour before the ships weighed anchor.

Rehearsal of this operation had been impossible except on paper, but careful study of it had produced instructions that were comprehensive, yet elastic enough for emergency. The order for the

SQUADRON FLAGSHIP "SAN FRANCISCO."
Receiving Mine Lighters Alongside in Inverness Firth.

operation gave a complete program, including a mining schedule showing the time when each ship was to begin laying and how many mines to plant. This was gone over with the captains, and then Captain H. R. Godfrey, R. N., and I had a conference with Rear Admiral Strauss, on the general features of the excursion. Captain Godfrey, commanding H. M. S. *Vampire* and the 14th Destroyer Flotilla, was our first escort leader.

Our operation was to be no "captains' fight." Teamwork was indispensable. Every ship must keep in her station throughout and do her allotted stint exactly on time. The instructions said, "Once begun, keep strictly to schedule times, regardless of the *omission* of signals or delay in them." Otherwise there would be gaps in the barrier, impossible to fill without waste of time and space, and mines would be brought back that should have been planted. Teamwork in the high degree wanted meant every man alive to his interest in the general result and sensible to his responsibility for his part in it. All would learn this in time, but it must be driven home beforehand. It was of utmost importance that the first operation should be an unquestionable success.

Accordingly, after making the preliminary inspection of each new ship, I spoke to each ship's company, partly to comment on their work so far, but chiefly to enlist the best efforts of each individual. Rumor and conjecture were the sources of all they had learned hitherto of the work ahead of them. Now they were told something of its magnitude and importance—that it had been regarded as doubtful of accomplishment, but their squadron commander had promised success in their name, promised the kind of success that comes only with the best teamwork throughout the ship and by all ships in the squadron. Every man should realize that now, in war, his utmost was called for, as never before in his life; that however simple and unimportant his duty might seem, it was his to do, and he was counted on not to be content that any other man's work should be better done, and that, in our work, prolonged through hours, the attention must never slacken— the 600th mine must be as carefully tended as the first. The men gave the closest attention—not an eye wavered, hardly a muscle moved—giving back such confidence that, on board the *Canonicus,* which I had found in fine condition, I could wind up with, " And when the last mine is out, the only signal I expect to send to you is ' *Canonicus* well done '! "

CHAPTER EIGHT

The First Minelaying Excursion

The eve of our first departure was drizzling and misty. Attempts for some advance sleep were of no avail—too much pressure had directly preceded. When 11 o'clock came without sign of the two ships due from the inner anchorage in Beauly Basin, we in the flagship wondered why. The tide was falling, another half hour passed—would they never come? Signals and radio failed to get through. Very soon, if not already, they would be unable to pass through the new dredged channel. At last, near midnight, they appeared. The pilots had been delayed through a misunderstanding on shore, in itself slight—but it was a narrow escape from being 10 hours late, which, on our first operation, would have made a bad impression, without and within.

The start is made without signals, all dark and noiseless on board, except for the rumbling chain as the ship gets underway. As the *San Francisco* heads out slowly, one after another the signal quartermaster reports the other ships underway and following. We take two-thirds speed now. The full number of lookouts are at their stations and warned to be alert, and the men are now sent to the battery, making a little stir for the moment, then quiet falls again. Fort George shows the signal for an open gate, we increase to standard speed, and as the second ship passes out through the submarine net, they all form single column astern and close up—to 500 yards apart. The rocky shore looms high and black on the left, not a single house light showing. On the offshore side, small patrol craft can be dimly seen, on watch against lurking danger. Fifteen minutes more and we see long, low forms slinking against the dark background of North Sutor. Those are the escort destroyers, going out to form a screen. Close following them we make out larger, higher, moving shadows—our detachment from the other base—one, two, three, four—*five! All there!* The detachments are so timed that they reach the junction buoy at the same moment, and the whole squadron stands on, without pause, together, 10 ships in two parallel columns, 500 yards apart. Ahead and on either side are four destroyers, 12 in all. No signals, no lights, no sound but quiet tones on the bridge and the swash of the water overside. Three miles along, the water deepens to 60 feet. A screened flash from the flagship to the opposite leader and the squadron, all together, slackens speed, to get out paravanes—those underwater, outrigger-like affairs which guard against anchored mines in one's path. Only a few minutes, then up each column comes the sign " yes," passed by ships in succession—another flash from the flagship, and we resume standard speed again, keeping on, out Moray Firth, through the one-mile wide channel, which is swept daily for mines.

THE MINE SQUADRON AT SEA.
Returning to Base After Laying the Ninth Minefield.

Off Pentland Skerries, near John O'Groat's House, we turn east, and here as we pass, the supporting force files out of Scapa Flow—six light cruisers, then a squadron of battle cruisers and another of four battleships, each squadron screened by six destroyers. Very impressive are these great ships, majestic in movement, as they sweep off to the southward and eastward, disappearing in the morning haze, which magnifies their towering bulk. We see them no more until next day but know they are there, on guard against raiders.

The British Minelaying Squadron is out, too, four ships with a joint capacity of 1300 mines, but we do not meet. Though protected by the same heavy squadrons, we work independently, in different areas. They are bound this time for the section near the Norway coast, Area C it is called, while we are to begin at the southeastern corner of the middle section, Area A, and work to the westward.

Straight over to Udsire we go, a small island off the Norway coast, the nearest good landmark from which to take a departure for the minelaying start point. We make Udsire Light near 11.30 p. m., close in to about 11 miles distance, turn north for a sufficient run to give a good fix, and then head off-shore. Accurate determination of the minefield's position is necessary for use in laying another field close by subsequently, and also for the safety of the vessels sweeping the mines up after the war. There must be steady steaming and steering, with a minimum of changing course—no hesitation, no trial moves, for neither the time at disposal nor the submarine risk will permit.

All goes smoothly until the turn to head off-shore, when one destroyer crosses too close under *San Francisco's* stern and cuts her "taut wire." This is fine piano wire, furnished in spools of 140 miles of wire, the whole weighing one ton. A small weight would anchor the end to the bottom, and then a mile of wire meant a mile over the ground without question.

The wire is soon started again, and as the *Baltimore* is running her wire on the other flank, and the weather is clear enough for good navigational bearings and star sights, no harm is done. We head for a position seven miles in advance of the start point, so that the squadron may turn together to the minelaying course and have still a half-hour in which to settle down.

It is a busy night and early morning, keeping the ships in formation, verifying the navigation, keeping a keen lookout in every direction for submarines—we are now in their regular route—going over the mines for final touches and making other preparations necessarily left to the last. About 4 o'clock, Lieut. Commander Cunningham, the flagship's navigator, reports that we shall reach the start point at 5.27 a. m. Captain Butler and I check his figures, and at 4.27 the signal is made that minelaying will begin in one hour. The crews go to mining stations, to see all clear and then stand by. In the flagship we watch for the reports of readiness. Ship by ship they signal in the affirmative. They are ready, every one.

Now the last turn has been made and the signal is flying to begin laying in seven minutes. The ships are formed in a single line abreast, speeding towards the start point—like race horses when the starter's flag is up. It is a stirring sight. How will it go, after all these months—for some of us years—of preparation? Our work to-day will mean much to those in Washington.

No ship is off the line by so much as a quarter length. Commander Canaga stands with watch in hand—"two minutes, one minute, thirty seconds, fifteen?" He looks up inquiringly. A nod—all right. "Five seconds—haul down!" Up go the red flags on the first ships to plant, the sign that their minelaying has begun, and word comes from the flagship's launching station at the stern, "First mine over." All well so far.

The minelaying now runs entirely by the time table. Each ship gives her successor five minutes warning and, as her last mine dives overboard, shows the signal "Begin minelaying at once; I have suspended." The successor begins accordingly, showing her red flag. The staff officers on board the *San Francisco* watch for these signals, comparing the times with what they should be, and counting also the seconds elapsed between the launching of successive mines, from the ships whose sterns we can see. A few seconds out now and then—otherwise all goes according to schedule, just as planned before leaving the United States.

The hardest task is on board the *Housatonic*—a new ship, with a new mining installation, of type untried in service, and a crew inexperienced in minelaying—dropping 675 mines without intermission, 1 every $11\frac{1}{2}$ seconds, during 2 hours and 10 minutes. Her mate is standing by, ready for any interruption, but the *Housatonic* completes the task without a break—making a world record, a continuous line of mines, 28 miles long. On a later occasion, the *Canonicus* planted 860 mines in 3 hours 35 minutes, an unbroken line of 43 miles.

About 20 minutes after planting began, an explosion was felt and a geyser seen astern. A few minutes later the same occurred again, and other explosions followed, at varying intervals and distances, some just visible on the horizon. Others which were nearer, as evidenced by the sharpness of the shock, threw up no geyser, indicating that they were at the middle or lowest depth.

In the proof tests held off Cape Ann in April, it had been observed that a mine at the middle level, 160 feet submergence, made no surface disturbance when detonated, until 8 seconds had elapsed, and then only as much as the wash of a light swell over a submerged rock. At the deepest level, 240 feet submergence, a detonation produced no more surface upheaval than there is in a glass of well iced champagne. The ship being about 800 yards away, the shock was heavy and sharp. The water surface all over could be seen to tremble with the shock, but directly over the mine itself, when, after 27 seconds, the gas came up, there was no more surface disturbance than a pleasure canoe could have ridden with safety. A slick on the water would follow, but this could not be distinguished at much over a mile distance nor at all if there were a white cap sea running.

Observers recorded the number, times, and approximate positions of all explosions and, on board the *San Francisco* and *Baltimore,* there were listeners stationed at the submarine signal receivers, so as to get a full count. All observers did not agree, as the indications from sounds and shocks varied according to distance and depth. Some explosions gave a prolonged reverberation, at times sounding to the unassisted ear like two or three explosions in rapid succession, but in the submarine signal receiver each explosion made a distinct sound, unmistakable.

The count by the *San Francisco* and *Baltimore,* differing by only 2, practically agreed on 100 explosions, or about 3 per cent of all mines planted. Although a perfect record was desirable, the detonations showed the minefield to be alive and sensitive, and their number was not large for a new mine, not yet long enough in service to refine out the minor defects.

Surprising enough on deck, where one could see, that first explosion must have startled the men in the engine room, in the coal bunkers, and on the lower mine decks. The blow rings sharper down there, where resulting damage, in broken pipe joints or started boiler tubes, might be expected first. Whether gun, torpedo, or mine, however, it is all one—the duties go on just the same.

As the mines on the launching deck move slowly aft, those on lower decks move forward, to the elevators and up. Working spaces are cramped, passages narrow, bulkhead doors closed wherever possible. At the right time, a door will be opened, the portable section of mine track adjusted, the mines in that compartment hauled out, and the door closed again water-tight, all as quickly as possible. Close, hot, foul with oily steam and sea-sickness—it is sweating, disagreeable work below decks. But complaint is nowhere in the ships. The feeling is well expressed by one man, writing home:

> When the first mine went over, I had a curious feeling of exultation. The fear, the perils, the uncertainties that surround our work, slipped from me like the foolish fancies of a nightmare. There, at last, was a nail in the Kaiser's coffin. Come what might, I had justified my existence. Had the whole German High Seas Fleet appeared in the offing, I am sure I should have gone to my battle station with a shout of glee.

Prolonged activity, in preparing the squadron and bringing it out, makes it trying now for me, to look on, hands folded—nothing to do while everything goes well—yet constantly alert, for instant decision in case of mishap. After nearly four hours, the schedule is finished. Some marker buoys are dropped, for later use in beginning another minefield. The line of ships then takes the narrower route formation, and we head back for the base. Butler, Canaga, and I exchange quiet congratulations. Our work together has been to good purpose.

The men clean up the decks, get a wash for themselves, and those off duty drop asleep—anywhere—the deck is covered with them. On top of the duties common to all men-of-war, to move the 400-ton masses of mines, in slow but steady time, is very fatiguing, even with steam winches to help.

We are not finished yet. Expectation of a quiet afternoon doze, handy to the bridge, is rudely dispelled by a smoke screen started by the destroyers. Unaware it is only an exercise, all hands tumble up to battle stations. Then one minelayer must stop, to tighten a nut working loose. Two destroyers are left to guard her, all three overtaking us in a few hours. Next a dirigible balloon heaves in sight, and then a widespread smoke covers the horizon, developing into a convoy of 50 vessels. Finally, in the midst of dinner, the siren of our next astern shrieks " Submarine to port!"

While the minelayers, upon signal, swing together away from the danger quarter, the *Vampire* swoops by at 30 knots, to drop two depth charges on the spot indicated. Captain Godfrey signals, " Whatever was there, those charges will keep him down for a

considerable time." All quiet again, we return to our cold prov-
ender, remarking that, as a name, mine squadron is ill chosen.
It should be " Crowded Hour Club."

Reports had now come in from all the ships that there had been
no casualties. All were prepared to undertake another operation
upon receiving the mines, and without further incident we returned to our former anchorages, arriving at 3.30 next morning.
But ere that day closed, so memorable in our lives, I signaled
the squadron:

The operation to-day was an excellent performance by each ship and by
the squadron as a whole. The fact of some premature explosions does not
detract from the highly creditable mine handling and steady steaming. Confidence in the personnel and faith in the undertaking are well justified, and
captains may well be proud of their commands, as the squadron commander
is of the squadron.

SQUADRON ORGANIZATION AND SHIPS' DATA

MINE SQUADRON ONE, U. S. ATLANTIC FLEET

(Designated in H. B. M. Grand Fleet, SECOND MINELAYING SQUADRON)

Captain Reginald R. Belknap, U. S. N., Squadron Commander

Flagship—U. S. S. *San Francisco*

Chief of staff.....................*Captain H. V. Butler.
Aid and tactical officer............. Commander B. L. Canaga.
Squadron construction and mining
    officer ....*Comdr. L. F. Kimball.
Squadron engineer ....*Lt. Comdr. F. R. Berg.
Squadron engineer from 1 October,
    1918 ....*Lieut. G. J. Blessing.
Flag lieutenant and secretary...... Lt. Comdr. E. S. R. Brandt.
Aid and secretary after 23 August,
    1918 .... Ensign Roger F. Hooper, R. F.
Squadron radio officer, also signal
    officer after 23 August, 1918.... Lieut. R. C. Starkey.
Communication officer and aid..... Lt. (j. g.) R. L. White, R. F.
Squadron surgeon ....*Lt. Comdr. G. C. Rhoades (M. C.).
Squadron surgeon from 1 October,
    1918 ....*Lieut. H. P. Stevens (M. C.), R. F.
Squadron supply officer...........*Lieut. C. R. Eagle (P. C.).
Squadron athletic officer..........*Lt. Comdr. G. W. Hewlett.
Assistant squadron construction offi-
    cer ....*Lieut. G. R. Arey (C. C.).

San Francisco (flagship)—Captain H. V. Butler, U. S. N.
    Launched at Union Iron Works, San Francisco, October 26, 1889, as
    a protected cruiser; commissioned as a mine ship August 21, 1911;
    length 324 feet, beam 49 feet, extreme draft 24 feet, full load displace-
    ment 4583 tons; twin screw, 18 knots; four 5-inch 51-caliber guns, two
    3-inch anti-aircraft guns, 170 mines; officers 22, crew 350; additional
    for flagship, officers 5, enlisted men 47; total on board 424.
Baltimore—Captain A. W. Marshall, U. S. N.
    Launched at Cramp's Shipyard, Philadelphia, October 26, 1888, as a
    protected cruiser; commissioned as a mine ship March 8, 1915; length

---

* Additional to ship duties.

335 feet, beam 48½ feet, extreme draft 24 feet, 5482 tons; twin screw, 18 knots; four 5-inch 51-caliber guns, two 3-inch anti-aircraft guns, 180 mines; officers 21, crew 339; total 360.

Roanoke—Captain C. D. Stearns, U. S. N.

Launched August 30, 1911, named *El Dia;* commissioned as a mine-layer January 25, 1918, at Tietjen and Lang's Shipyard, Hoboken, N. J.

Housatonic—Captain J. W. Greenslade, U. S. N.

Launched November 14, 1899, named *El Rio;* commissioned January 25, 1918, at Tietjen and Lang's.

Canandaigua—Captain W. H. Reynolds, U. S. N.

Launched in May, 1901, named *El Siglo;* commissioned March 2, 1918, at the Morse Dry Dock and Repair Company, Brooklyn, N. Y.

Canonicus—Captain T. L. Johnson, U. S. N.

Launched November 14, 1899, named *El Cid;* commissioned March 2, 1918, at the Morse Yard.

All four preceding were built at the Newport News Ship and Engine Building Company, Newport News, Va., as freight liners for the Southern Pacific Steamship Company (Morgan Line). Length 405 feet, beam 48 feet, draft 20 feet, displacement 7000 tons; single screw, 15 knots; one 5-inch 51-caliber gun aft, two 3-inch anti-aircraft guns forward; 830 mines normally, 900 maximum, carried on three decks; officers 21, crew 400; total 421.

Quinnebaug—Commander D. Pratt Mannix, U. S. N.

Launched October 14, 1898, named *Jefferson;* commissioned as mine-layer March 23, 1918, at Robins' Dry Dock and Repair Company, Brooklyn, N. Y.

Saranac—Captain Sinclair Gannon, U. S. N.

Launched in 1899, named *Hamilton;* commissioned April 9, 1918, at James Shewan & Sons, Inc., Brooklyn.

Both were built by John Roach & Sons, Chester, Pa., as coast-wise passenger and freight liners for the Old Dominion Steamship Company; length 375 feet, beam 42 feet, draft 18½ feet, displacement 5150 tons; single screw, 16 knots; one 5-inch 51-caliber gun aft, two 3-inch anti-aircraft guns forward; mines 612 normally, 642 maximum, carried on two decks; officers 18, crew 392; total 410.

Shawmut—Captain W. T. Cluverius, U. S. N.

Aroostook—Captain J. Harvey Tomb, U. S. N.

Both vessels were launched in 1907 at Cramp's Shipyard, Philadelphia, named *Massachusetts* and *Bunker Hill* respectively; commissioned as minelayers at Navy Yard, Boston, Mass., December 7, 1917; length 387 feet, beam 52 feet, draft 17½ feet, displacement 3800 tons; twin screw, oil fuel, 20 knots; one 5-inch 51-caliber and one 3-inch anti-aircraft gun on the middle line aft, one 3-inch anti-aircraft gun forward; 320 mines normally, 352 maximum, all carried on one deck; officers 20, crew 346; total 366.

4

Totals of Squadron:

Tonnage, 54,000 tons.

Mines, normal 5530, maximum 5834.

Officers 208, men 3839; total 4047.

In addition, four sea-going tugs belonged to the squadron, as described in Chapter 22.

CHAPTER NINE

ATHLETICS

A shortage of some mine parts that had encountered difficulty in manufacture now delayed the preparation for a second excursion, and the respite came opportunely, for we had been driving hard for some time.

Though the minelayers were comfortable enough to live in when empty, it was quite different with mines on board. Then only a few of the men could swing their hammocks, the others having to lie on the decks. Crowding the mess tables together, horns and sharp corners ever ready to tear the clothes, mines were constantly at one's elbow, and everywhere were mine tracks, half-knee high, or turntables, to trip the unwary or bark his shin. No smoking was allowed below decks, and the space above decks was very limited for crews so numerous. The men made no complaint—such men will not complain of discomfort which seems temporary and unavoidable, when incident to an undertaking that interests them—but since the discomfort could not be alleviated but, on the contrary, would increase with the frequency of excursions and with inclement weather, sufficient diversion was imperative to maintain the fine, cheerful spirit which had characterized the work so far.

Let the report on squadron athletics, written at the end of September by Ensign Walter P. Hanson, U. S. N. R. F., editor of our *Athletic Bulletin,* tell what was done, in true sporting page style:

The situation was new, practically unparallelled, and called for immediate action. With the exception of the *San Francisco* and *Baltimore,* none of the ships had the traditional atmosphere of a man-of-war, so essential to the building up of *esprit de corps.* It was a new squadron, manned largely by new men, performing a new operation in strange waters. Something was needed to weld this war-sprouted organization into a solid, indissoluble unit, to build up ship spirit and a high squadron spirit, recalling old traditions and laying the foundation for new ones, to fire the men's enthusiasm to a pitch that would insure the success of the gigantic operation in hand and spell defeat for the German submarine forces.

There were other just as important reasons why an athletic organization was necessary. Minelaying in contested waters is not the easiest nor the least dangerous of duties. To eat, sleep and work in close proximity to tons of the deadliest explosive known, and then to cruise day and night in submarine infested waters with this same explosive for cargo—knowing that one well-aimed torpedo, a well-placed mine, or a few enemy shells, would wipe out an entire ship's company, and possibly the whole squadron—is not exactly the sort of recreation a worn-out business man would seek as a cure for "nerves." And blue-jackets, despite a common fallacy in America, are no more than human. Numerous mining excursions, with no intervening periods of recreation, were bound to tell on the men.

Relaxation and amusement they would get in one form or another. Where were they to turn for it? To the theaters and amusement centers of two Scotch, war-stricken villages? They were almost a myth and couldn't hold a man-sized blue-jacket's attention for half an hour a week. What then—the Y. M. C. A.? Yes, to some extent, but even those faithful workers couldn't solve the problem. Active amusement the men wanted, excitement, thrills, anything to take their minds off their work for a few hours several times a week when they went ashore.

Obviously there was but one answer to the question and that was the healthful recreation of organized, competitive athletics. Athletics of all sorts and forms, teams organized on each ship, and an officially recognized and governed organization to direct the activities of the entire squadron. Spirited competition and clean sportsmanship was to be the keynote of the movement, with one directing head, under the supervision of the Squadron Commander.

The official "season" was formally opened on July 4, at both bases, with eight teams competing. The initial success was most gratifying. The spirit shown by the townspeople gave the day all the ear-marks of a regular league opening in the states. The games were closely contested and the players, cheered on by the rooting of hundreds of loyal "fans," displayed an excellent brand of ball. Business houses had declared a holiday in honor of our Independence Day and apparently the natives decided to attend the festivities in a body, for at Inverness more than three thousand of them were present, eagerly attempting to learn the intricacies of the game.

From then on, the success of athletics in the squadron was assured. When the ships were in port and the weather permitted, not a day passed without one or more games played. Each team was loyally supported by its own ship's company, even the officers forgetting their dignity long enough to root long and loudly. In these demonstrations the men were moderate, considerate of the neighbors, realizing that local custom did not favor such noise, though indulged now with perfect good humor, since we appeared to need it.

Athletic activities were not confined to baseball. Boat-racing, track, tug-of-war teams, boxing and wrestling, were all taken up and encouraged. On July 4, the entire morning was given over to boat racing. Excellent time was made over the mile course and good seamanlike qualities were displayed. The afternoon track events developed into a spirited contest, in which the marks made would have done justice to any first-class American university. Again on Labor Day a similar athletic meet was arranged

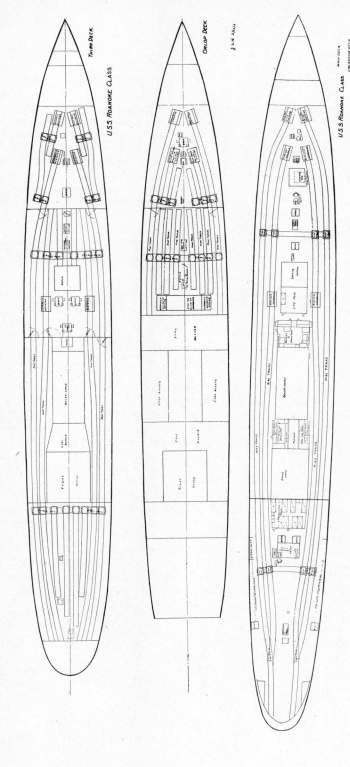

ARRANGEMENT OF MINE TRACKS, ELEVATORS, AND TURNTABLES, IN "ROANOKE" CLASS OF MINELAYERS.

and once more the same measure of success was attained, thousands of townspeople in attendance.

Boxing and wrestling were taken up by the individual ships and, generally speaking, one evening each week was given over to "happy hours," for bouts in the ring and on the mat. Ambitious youngsters would send forth bristling challenges, which were immediately snapped up by rivals in other ships and the resulting encounter was the equivalent—seldom bloodless—of a naval engagement in building up *esprit de corps*.

Excellent golf courses and tennis courts lay convenient to both bases, and many a day the Squadron Commander returned from the Nigg links with 18 officers crowding the barge. The squadron surgeon, Dr. Rhoades, secured many recruits for the ancient and honorable game, with the result that upward of 50 officers out of 200 entered the tournament played in September.

From the start the good effect on the men was noticeable. A consistently winning baseball team made that ship's company the envy of all others, and fostered a spirit that could not confine itself to athletics alone but was injected into drills, mining excursions and all forms of ship's work. Indeed, it would not be overshooting the mark to state that the success of the operation as a whole was due in large part to the spirit of enthusiasm aroused among the men by organized competitive athletics.

The men and officers were benefited from a mental and moral, as well as physical, standpoint. They had something really interesting to go to see on shore and to talk about on returning aboard. Their minds were taken absolutely away from war while the games were in progress, their nerves relaxed and the tension removed. Their activities were directed into healthful channels, whereas, thrown upon their own resources, they might have sought amusement in some harmful form.

Not only did athletics benefit the men, it also played its part from an international aspect, especially baseball. Essentially an American sport, it typifies everything American—rapid thinking, quickness of action, and purely American individualism, coupled with the keenest alertness in teamwork. These traits the British admire in the "Yanks." At any of our baseball games, hundreds of British soldiers and sailors could always be seen, wearing broad grins of appreciation and admiration of the cleverness of their comrades in arms. So much were they taken up with the sport that on some British ships they began to organize baseball teams, with the hope in the near future to compete with their American cousins. And the small boys in the towns were quick to take up playing ball with a stick and an old string ball. All this helped in creating a spirit of cooperation and good feeling between the British and the Americans, so important to both present and future common aims.

CHAPTER TEN

THE SQUADRON COMPLETE

After a conference with the commanding officers with the various incidents of the first excursion fresh in mind, revised instructions applying equally to every excursion were drawn up, to be supplemented by the particulars for each successive occasion issued at the appropriate time. The term excursion met with ready adoption, for its cheerful suggestion of a return—weary no doubt, but content.

A navigation memorandum of the intended courses, speeds, and principal incidents, for the information of the escort leader and each ship, accompanied the excursion order. An excellent understanding, as well as good feeling, grew up between the squadron and its escort. The escort commander would often dine on board the *San Francisco* and discuss the coming excursion and the two bodies soon came to move as one, changing course, night or day, or changing formation, frequently with only a whistle blast—a whole excursion sometimes without any tactical signal at all between the two bodies, except for some unforeseen change of course or speed.

Preparations had begun at once for the second excursion to continue the first minefield, but change had become necessary, and a line across Area C was ordered—not, however, until *Roanoke* had been loaded with 830 mines of an adjustment not suited to the changed plan, and these remained on board 33 days, the crew living around, but keeping up cleanliness and order the same as usual. So long a period fully loaded had not been contemplated, but it showed one more thing these vessels could do when well manned and commanded.

As before, assembly was at night 30 June, and Udsire the point of final departure. The supporting force was the 6th Battle Squadron of five American battleships under Rear Admiral Hugh Rodman, U.S.N. Needless to say, every one came on deck to see our handsome battle squadron, as it filed out past Pentland Skerries and formed line, disappearing to the south-eastward. Twice during the afternoon submarine periscopes were seen by the battleships and their destroyer screen, which opened fire and dropped depth bombs, but without known effect.

Considerable current was found near the Norwegian coast, but visibility was good until we passed to the northward of Udsire; then it became increasingly hazy. The run of the flagship, guiding, was accurately determined notwithstanding, by other marks to the northward before they too became indistinct. At 4.26 a. m., minelaying began—great care taken not to lay any mines inside Norwegian waters, yet to begin just outside them. Despite the unexpected strong current at the critical moment, the first mines were dropped within 250 yards of the intended spot, just outside the three-mile limit.

Overcast sky prevented obtaining good observations to check the run during the minelaying, and as there was no check on latitude and the current was variable, the course was changed slightly for the last third of the run, to be sure of clearing our first field, towards which we were heading. This accounts for the bend in that line on the chart. We were crossing the 150-fathom deep water which skirts the Norway coast, three large ships, *Canonicus, Canandaigua,* and *Housatonic,* led by *San Francisco,* laying 2200 mines in two rows on a line 46 miles long. In spite of repeated breaking of the distance-measuring taut wire, the speed over ground was estimated closely enough to end the line within one-half mile of the point intended, which was correct within 1 per cent.

There were again no casualties and all the mines were planted. Two ships planted 710 each in continuous strings, fully establishing the success of the mining installations. There was no longer any doubt of the ability of one of these ships to plant her entire load of 860 mines without break. All vessels returned to base ready for further duty.

The explosions of defective mines on this excursion amounted to between 4 and 5 per cent, and reports received from British trawlers watching the first minefield indicated that enough more had gone off in that field since the first day, to bring the total there up to between 5 and 6 per cent. Despite all remedy, these explosions increased in number up to the 5th excursion. Then the cause was found to be due not to unskilful, negligent, or otherwise faulty procedure in either the ships or the bases, but to lie partly in supersensitiveness in the mines' adjustment, partly in imperfection in manufacture—inevitable in such large numbers made under prevailing industrial conditions, especially of a new design.

On June 29, just before departure on the second excursion, the minelayers *Shawmut,* Captain W. T. Cluverius, *Aroostook,* Commander J. H. Tomb, and *Saranac,* Commander Sinclair Gannon, and the repair ship *Black Hawk,* Captain R. C. Bulmer, had arrived from the United States. Uncompleted work had not delayed them like the others, but the trial runs of the *Shawmut* and *Aroostook* showed their fuel consumption to be much larger than had been estimated—no data having been available when their conversion was planned—making their fuel capacity insufficient for the passage over. Indefinite delay, until a tanker could accompany them, was averted by the captains hunting up enough oil hose to fuel the ships at sea. Their departure on June 16 took place during the German submarines' activity on the New England coast—not a favorable condition for ships just out of a navy yard. Twice during the crossing, the *Black Hawk* took the *Shawmut* and *Aroostook* in tow, to give them fuel oil. Though a new operation to all hands—likewise new ships, new crews, half a gale of wind, and oil hose twice as heavy as proper—it was done well, without mishap, and all four arrived at our bases ready for service.

The third excursion could therefore be made by the full squadron of ten. It was to continue the first minefield, and as some of our mark buoys were known to have broken adrift—we had passed two on the second excursion—the flagship's navigator, Lieut. Commander Cunningham, was sent out in the squadron tugs *Patuxent* and *Patapsco,* to verify what might remain of the buoyfield. Finding half the buoys in place, he planted two new ones as a precaution. Then he passed along both our minefields, listening for further explosions, but heard none. The necessary improvement in the buoy moorings was now made, so effectively that they could be counted on thereafter. Each ship carried four buoys on her quarters, ready to drop on the instant. One stroke of an axe, or pull on a slip would release a buoy and its 1000-lb. sinker together, the mooring wire cable being so looped up around the buoy as to pay out clear. Thus the ship had no need to reduce speed nor any fear of getting her screw foul of the buoy.

Embarking mines for the third excursion had already begun when a message came that no mines were to be placed west of zero longitude for the present, a restriction that shortened the intended line by 30 miles, quite upsetting the embarking arrangements then in progress.

Meantime, the original plan had, in London, undergone considerable modification as to the constitution of the barrage. Originally of three systems, each comprising three lines of mines—upper, middle, and lower levels—the necessity which had developed for wider spacing between mines, to avoid structural damage to neighboring mines when one was detonated—300 feet instead of 150, as originally planned—made it seem desirable to increase the number of lines of mines, so as to maintain the same density of the mine barrage as a whole. The revision aimed to increase the risk to surface passage considerably. No effective patrol being maintained along the barrage, submarines would naturally prefer the surface. The revised plan, in brief, made 10 upper level rows instead of 3, and 4 middle and 4 lower level, instead of 3 each, or a total of 18 rows instead of 9.

Rather than shorten our line and again employ only part of the squadron, the Commander of the Mine Force took up the revised scheme at once, ordering 5400 mines prepared, for a field of 5 parallel lines 54 miles long. All 10 ships were loaded nearly to full capacity, *Housatonic* taking 840 mines. Departure was taken at 2 p. m., Sunday 14 July, hauling down, as we got underway, the dress bunting which had been hoisted in honor of the French Bastille Day.

CHAPTER ELEVEN

Tactics

Ten ships laden with high explosive, navigating in mine-swept channels, in submarine thoroughfares, and near minefields beyond sight of fixed marks—compactness of the minefield demanding that the layers steam as near together as safe—necessity for keeping together in fog, darkness, or submarine attack—these were the conditions governing our tactics.

Thus, the mining excursions were not merely arduous in preparation and execution. Precision and quickness of action while at sea were imperative, from start to finish. To foster these, a steady tension was kept up throughout the squadron, a tension which likewise helped the individual ships to maintain a careful habit among the men, without making them jumpy or fearful. To sustain attention and prevent over-confidence growing with familiarity, unremitting pains were exercised to note and correct any irregularity or apparent slackness—not to find fault but to keep things taut everywhere. Only in this way could compliance with all details be insured—so very important in our work.

From assembly at the buoy until the return to it after the excursion, the *San Francisco,* leading the squadron, would maintain a steady pace, sometimes increasing to make up for adverse current, but rarely slackening speed for anything. The squadron's position was frequently compared with the time schedule, and no effort was spared to carry through the excursion with precision. There was time enough, we had speed enough, but none too much of either, and the whole body felt a constant urge towards a direct and clean-cut movement out to the field, over it, and back to the base.

Stretched in two mile-long columns while in mine-searched waters, which were comparatively narrow, the formation would widen and shorten upon reaching the 50-fathom line, so as to diminish the depth of the target offered to a submarine. Approaching the mine start point, the vessels would take the relative positions which they would occupy when the mining was begun—not too soon, because such a formation was unwieldy, and if maneuvering into position involved much turning, the formation would become disordered. The 10 vessels were of 5 different types, with different handling qualities and having very small speed reserve with which to regain lost position. On the other hand, the change had to be made early enough for all vessels to get settled in station, at standard speed, before the minelaying began.

As the planting progressed, we had to make use of large, lighted, navigation buoys, planted in the open sea, obviously for our use. The British had warned us, from their own experience, of the enemy's habit of moving all such buoys whenever seen, or planting mines near them—sometimes doing both. Working far away from the nearest landmark, we would pass close to these buoys in order to determine the position of the mine start point accurately. Against enemy mines which might be around the buoys, our paravanes were counted upon for protection, but here came in a complication. While paravanes would protect against ordinary mines, they actually increased the risk from any of our own mines which they might touch. To keep the paravanes out until after clearing the buoy, then take them in before approaching one of our fields, would have been simple enough, but for the necessity of maintaining steady speed and course from the buoy to the mining start point, which precluded slowing down to take the paravanes in. Since the risk could be measured from our own mines but not from the enemy's, the paravanes were always kept in use.

Pressure of time and division of the ships between two bases while in port limited the tactical training of the squadron to what could be done while crossing the Atlantic and while going to and from the minefields. The special equipment to facilitate accurate station keeping which is usually found in men-of-war was lacking in these ex-merchant vessels. They had comparatively small rudders, and the nice regulation of steam to the engines, necessary for steady steaming in company, was very difficult with their deficient means for that purpose. Moreover, on the first excursion by the complete squadron of 10 vessels, 4 of them took part for the first time. The excellent performance of the squadron as a whole was all the more remarkable.

Passing through the mark buoys, which the sloop H. M. S. *Laburnum* pointed out, the squadron, formed in three lines abreast,

stood on beyond, to allow distance in which to steady down on
the reverse course, then turned ships 90 degrees right together, by
divisions in succession. This evolution formed the squadron in a
single column which steered about SSW, until within two miles
of the previous minefield. Two of the 10 vessels were on the
right flank, so that a second, simultaneous turn, ships right,
brought the squadron into the planting formation, consisting of a
line of 8 ships abreast, stretching a mile and three-quarters, the
remaining two in an advance line, 500 yards ahead, with three

THE SQUADRON IN MINELAYING FORMATION.
Two Ships of British Minelaying Squadron in the Left Background.

miles still to go, allowing 15 minutes time in which to settle
down, before the order to begin planting. The execution of the
operation was seamanlike to a degree, and the alignment, distance keeping, and handling of the vessels, in approaching and on
the planting line, were excellent throughout.

It would have widened the field unnecessarily to dispose all 10
ships abreast. The advanced ships would ease back into the main
line as soon as two of the 8 ships directly astern had finished their
minelaying and speeded ahead, leaving vacancies. Ample time
was allowed to do this slowly, before their time came to plant,
so as to avoid the extra demand on their engines which might
be caused by dropping back too fast. The ships were neither new
nor decrepit, but there was no excuse for taking unnecessary

chances of spoiling a good performance by the squadron as a whole. Steady steaming and steering were important for safety—as well as for regularity of the mine-spacing. God help a ship whose engine broke down or rudder jammed during the mine-laying! With a strong head wind, she would drift into the mine-field, before even a destroyer could tow her clear. It was partly for such an emergency that the sweepers originally included with our force were wanted—powerful, handy, seagoing tugs, able to assist in any circumstances. The tugs that we had were not fast enough to keep up with the squadron. Fortunately, engine or steering disablement never occurred during planting, but two did occur just afterward, and once, in Fair Island Channel, on the way to plant, a ship had to stop for a disabled feed pump. It was 11 o'clock at night, pitch dark, with the tide turning strong towards the 9th minefield, and in the submarines' thoroughfare. As I slowed the squadron and waited for report of the probable length of delay, I felt what a reliance a good tender would have been!

The support force on the third excursion, the 4th Battle Squadron, came close enough to observe the minelaying, steaming along parallel, four miles distant, for an hour. Its commander, in H. M. S. *Hercules,* was Vice Admiral Sir Montague E. Browning, who, with the French Rear Admiral Grasset, had come from Bermuda in the earliest days of our entering the war, to attend the first conference on our naval participation, and as their flagships, H. M. S. *Leviathan* and the *Jeanne d'Arc,* stood in to Hampton Roads, the *San Francisco* had been the vessel to salute their flags. Now, in the same ship, it was a pleasure to lead a large, new mine squadron, performing so creditably before such an observer, the more so as Admiral Browning had sent a special message of welcome upon our arrival from America.

After this excursion was over and all the reports were in from the several ships, showing that all mines had been planted, with no mishaps of any kind, and that the vessels were ready to undertake another excursion, the following signal was sent:

The squadron commander extends sincere congratulations upon the completion of to-day's mining operation by the whole squadron. It was a handsome performance that would have done credit to a squadron of long experience. The squadron commander, the captains, the officers, and every man may rightly feel deep pride in having earned a success worthy of our navy's best traditions. 7.45 p. m., 15 July, 1918.

CHAPTER TWELVE

Some Incidents

By consensus of opinion, the limit of safe approach to a mine-field in the open sea was five miles. Where appreciable current exists, a heavy sea may cause mines to step along, or " migrate "— there is no telling how far—and the danger from mines adrift is naturally greater near a minefield than elsewhere. Mines are designed to become safe on breaking adrift and many of them are, but far from all. Submergence in salt water may derange the mechanism for that safety purpose. There was very little current across Area A, however, and the fine tactical qualities shown by the squadron lent confidence that it could be safely conducted much nearer to our minefields than five miles. Since the barrage plan had been revised, this closer approach had become necessary, if we were to get the whole barrage in between the southernmost line, already laid, and the northern limit, which had been publicly proclaimed. There was some aversion to proclaiming a new limit and we had no mind to say it was necessary. So, instead of lapping the ends of adjacent minefields, the practice was adopted of " butting " the new field close to the end of its neighbor, thus continuing the same line with only a small gap between adjacent ends.

Our first news of damage inflicted on the enemy came in mid-July, soon after the second excursion, though the barrier was then hardly more than begun. The information was authentic but not very circumstantial—the standing policy was against that. Four submarines were mentioned. One of them lost nearly all her fuel and called by wireless for help, so loudly that it was overheard and a British force was sent out to capture or destroy her—but too late. Another German submarine had come to her aid, and the two got safely back. Further details are lacking.

The third excursion, together with the British minefields in Area C, completed the equivalent of one system, extending from the Norway coast as far west as o degrees longitude. The prohibition against laying any mines farther westward than that was still in force—although the enemy submarines had changed their route so as to pass clear to the westward of the partial barrier. So our fourth excursion began a second " system," parallel to and five miles distant from the first.

Leaving the bases during the night of 28 July, and taking final departure from Buoy No. 2, which marked the north end of the division between Areas A and C, we ran south, clearing the ends of three British deep minefields by three miles—quite safe to do if they were all in their intended places. Then, by an " isodromic " maneuver—not easy and little favored, on account of the precision that is requisite, but necessary on this occasion—our three columns, with *San Francisco* making a fourth on the left, formed a single line to the right, of eight ships, with two more in an advanced line, all steering about WSW. Being on the outside of the turn, the old *San Francisco* had to spring from 12 to 16½ knots within a few minutes, to gain her station on the southern flank in time, but no parade ground evolution could have been done more smoothly, and the quickness with which all ships steadied into accurate distance and bearing showed that, in future, the steadying interval could be safely reduced. Originally a half hour, it was cut down to 75 seconds.

Commander Moir, a new escort leader, in H. M. S. *Valhalla,* smiled slightly as he read over the mining order for the first time and I asked whether it were about this isodromic movement. He replied, No; he was wondering how they could execute one of the intermediate changes which the order prescribed to be made en route, to sort the ships out from the assembling order to the arrangement which they would be in preparatory to swinging into minelaying formation. It did look mixed at first glance, there was no denying, but I said, " Watch them do it, the Rules of the Road will govern "—and when the time came, I felt quite willing for any one to be a witness.

At the end of a minefield, the wing and the center ships simultaneously would drop mark buoys, 250 yards from the last mines, and again one mile farther on, making in all six buoys in two lines. When we came back after 10 days or so, to continue that field, a destroyer would go well ahead, to sight and stand by the outermost buoy, and the flagship would lead for it, but not steer towards the minefield side of it until the inner line of buoys had been sighted—those which were only 250 yards from the mines. The outer buoys were regarded with suspicion until some of the

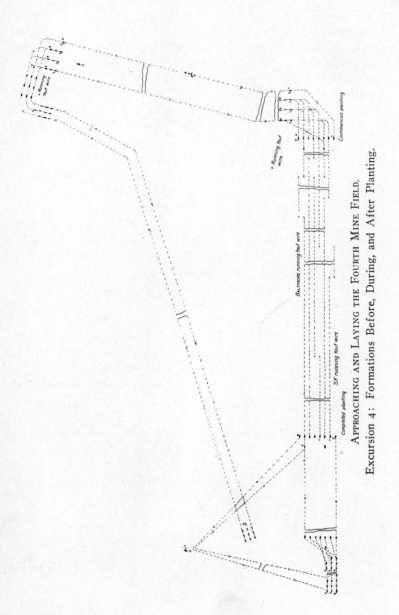

APPROACHING AND LAYING THE FOURTH MINE FIELD.

Excursion 4: Formations Before, During, and After Planting.

inner ones were seen to be in place. It was then deemed safe to lead between the two lines of buoys, for as long as there were any between the ships and the minefield, ships would be at least 250 yards clear. Passing in column midway between the lines of buoys to make the start, and allowing for the simultaneous turn into line abreast, the squadron could begin mining by the time the outer buoys were passed, thus leaving a gap of but little more than a mile between the mines in the old field and those in its continuation.

An early care while fitting out had been to organize and train a good lookout service. This duty is a severe tax on the men, and when, time after time, they see nothing suspicious, they tend to relax. Fearing this, as we had yet seen no submarines, barring an alarm on the first excursion, a special warning to lookouts was issued, which, fortunately was well supported on our next trip. A beautiful, peaceful evening off the Orkneys was rudely interrupted by messages from three different sources within the space of a minute, reporting a submarine estimated to be a half-hour ahead of us, outbound, making for Fair Island Channel. Taking no chances on its having innocent intentions towards us, Captain Godfrey turned his flank destroyers outward and bang! bang! went four depth charges, and four more on the other side—just to let the sub know he might except a hearty reception. The *Aroostook's* siren then shrieked for "torpedo to starboard!" the ship charging ahead across another's bows, and the *Housatonic's* steering chain took that occasion to break. Serenity was gone, for a time at least, but being in a swept channel, there was small choice for maneuvering. All we could do was to shorten up our formation before dark shut in and trust to our escort and a good lookout.

In the event of a submarine appearing, our rôle was to make off, leaving the attack to the destroyers and being careful not to harm them by our own fire. The escort was prepared to engage its own kind, as well as submarines, and even to make a sacrifice attack on light cruisers, to assist our escape under cover of a smoke screen, but our moderate speed—15 knots at best when keeping together— and the small number and caliber of our guns, made us rather helpless against an enemy cruiser's long-range, 6-inch gunfire and high speed.

Upon returning from an Allied conference in Malta on mining the Mediterranean, Rear Admiral Strauss came out with the squadron, on the seventh excursion, 26 August, hoisting his flag in the *San Francisco*. This was the first time our program was interfered with by fog, which shut in thick soon after assembly. Incidentally, our tug *Patuxent,* going out ahead with her sister *Patapsco* to observe, found herself in the midst of a large convoy from Norway that night and had a collision, which fortunately was not serious to either vessel.

After four hours' delay by fog, we made our departure buoy and steered for the end of the 5th minefield, 13 miles distant. Fog shut in again when we were half way, but fortunately lifted just before we should have had to turn back, and minelaying began, although the weather was still far from settled. Twice during the schedule, dense fog enveloped us, but the planting went on without interruption. It was rather ghostly to hear and feel the explosions of the defective mines, yet see nothing—not even the neighboring ship. Several times Admiral Strauss expressed admiration for the steady alignment of the formation, and upon leaving the *San Francisco* when we had returned to port, he signalled, " The Commander Mine Force congratulates Mine Squadron One on the seamanlike manner in which the seventh excursion was accomplished by all ships."

On this occasion, for the first and only time, one ship had to drop out from an excursion, the *Saranac* having a smash inside the cylinder of her main circulating pump shortly after the squadron had assembled. Temporary repairs being impossible soon enough, she returned to base. The absence of her 580 mines left the 7th minefield incomplete, and to make good the defect a special excursion was ordered for the *Shawmut,* Captain Cluverius, and *Aroostook,* Captain Tomb, the two fast minelayers.

Met off Cromarty buoy at 6 a. m., 31 August, by Commander Lowry in H. M. S. *Wrestler,* with three other destroyers, the detachment proceeded, first at 15 then at 17 knots, by the usual route to the end buoys of the seventh field, then close along the northern side of the field. The *Baltimore* had been on that flank, and after planting all her mines had dropped a buoy and again, at about 9-mile intervals, two other buoys, while steaming 500 yards abeam of the nearest planting vessel. A fresh breeze was now blowing, making the buoys none too easy to pick up. Fog had prevailed while the *Baltimore* was dropping the buoys, making uncertainty as to their position and also as to whether they were there at all. Accordingly, the detachment first ran parallel to the minefield, from 1000 to 2000 yards outside the line of buoys, so as to sight them all; then it turned back and began planting, *Shawmut* first. The mines were laid in one line averaging 600 yards outside the line of buoys, or about 1100 yards from the nearest line of mines, thus completing the original field neatly without wasting space. The mining installations of these fast ships worked as well at 17 knots as they had at 12, and altogether the excursion gave the two a good try out. They were back in their berths 26 hours after leaving them, in ample time to embark their mines for the squadron's next excursion, and with a record to their credit for laying 580 mines on the closest parallel to a deep-sea minefield that had ever been run.

CHAPTER THIRTEEN

Signals

Signals had come well to the front in the course of the first excursions, not only for tactics but also for assembling data quickly, so that a fairly comprehensive report of the excursion might go to headquarters by the first boat to shore after arrival. Spelling out messages by Morse or semaphore proved too slow and inaccurate for reports from nine ships in one afternoon, often in hazy weather, so a collection of phrases, and questions to be answered by reference number, was established, to be signaled by hoists of flags.

As we had expected to use the British signal system, a special training class was formed at Newport in January, while the mine-layers were fitting out. In consequence, from first falling in with British destroyers, the *San Francisco* communicated easily, and British flags could be used on the first excursion. But neither the British system nor our own was found to suit our needs, and to combine British flags with American meanings made a risk of misinterpretation at a critical time. So the American flags were restored to use and the British ones discontinued, except a few retained by each ship for calls and other routine uses, while the flagship kept a full set, for communicating with the escort by the British code. A new system, embodying several of the British features, was devised, mainly by Lieut. Commander E. S. R. Brandt, then flag lieutenant, and was put into effect on the second excursion. The main feature was that the meaning of tactical signals—those which required immediate action, affecting the ships' movements—was self-evident to anyone who knew the names of the flags.

Flags and associations already familiar having been utilized, the signalmen quickly learned. Separation among three anchorages prevented signal practice by the squadron as a whole in port, but drills several times daily at each anchorage and on the way out to the mining ground enabled the new code to be used on the full squadron's first trip. Great interest was evident among the signal forces of all ships. Signals were habitually hoisted only just long enough, as determined by experience, for the average vessel to repeat the hoist.   Competition became keen not to be the cause of delay, and very soon the signaling attained an accuracy, rapidity, and style comparing favorably with the best performance of any type of vessel.   Once or twice the *Quinnebaug*—whose mast was not high—beat the flagship in getting her own signal up to the yardarm.   Less than a minute by day, and often only 30 seconds, would suffice between giving an order for a tactical signal and beginning its execution by the squadron—without a glance at a key book or card at either end.   Most efficient telephone service would hardly equal that.

The *Vampire* soon picked up our new system, so that signals to her could frequently be dispensed with.   Upon one of ours going up, the corresponding British signal on *Vampire* would be seen in a few moments.

Accuracy of transmission and of record being very important where so much was done by signal, these were stimulated by daily comparison of the signal records of all ships.   A " discrepancy " sheet was compiled, to show the errors and omissions of each ship for the previous day, and directly after each excursion, the signal officers would meet, to compare the signal records of the trip. A further check was kept by a staff officer being constantly on watch on board the *San Francisco* when at sea, taking notes upon incidents and errors in signals, station-keeping, and the behavior of ships.   The Recording Angel could not have been more observant.   I would edit the rough record at the end of a watch, references to the pertinent instructions were entered, and a smooth " Discrepancy Report " was sent to all ships at the end of the excursion, as a reminder of their sins.

Had the signal officers been regulars and but one system of signals been in use from the beginning, the high standard maintained would have been commendable.   The attainment of such a standard by inexperienced personnel, adopting a new system on very short notice, was highly creditable to all concerned. Especially should there be mention of Chief Quartermaster William H. Kerins, of the *San Francisco,* and the other chiefs, whose training and management of their signalmen and whose own skill and fidelity made our quick and accurate communication possible.

CHAPTER FOURTEEN
THE BARRIER ACROSS

The barrage began to show results early in July, after our second excursion, although not yet half across. The enemy submarines changed their route then, so as to go through Fair Island Channel, south instead of north of the Shetlands. Thus they would pass west of the partial barrage, through the 60-mile wide passage still open. The fact of Area A having been proclaimed gave ample warning, and even the enemy could not complain of being ambushed, if he sustained damage there. Advertising a minefield two months in advance was certainly fair play. But now came the mining of Area B, which would carry the barrier clear across the last 45 miles of the 230-mile stretch. This was not published, but the enemy might have assumed that it would be done sooner or later.

A joint excursion by the two squadrons was arranged, Rear Admiral Strauss commanding the whole, flying his flag on board *San Francisco* again. The squadrons joined off the middle Orkneys the morning of 7 September, and began the minelaying a few miles to the northward, starting from a buoy placed by H. M. S. *Laburnum* and removed by her after we had passed. As we were directly in the submarines' thoroughfare, special patrols were provided, surface and air, in Fair Island Channel and also well to the southward of us. The American squadron planted six upper level lines, the British squadron planted one similar line, after the completion of which it separated to the southward, returning to its base at Grangemouth, Firth of Forth. On the way, one of them had a collision in the fog with a destroyer of its escort, which later sank in consequence.

Our squadron turned north at the end of our minefield, ran taut wire to Buoy No. 5, thence paralleled the minefield at five miles distance for observation of defective mine explosions, steering west to the Orkneys and returning to the base on the reverse of the outbound courses. Fog came on soon after mining was finished, continuing intermittently until we made port. For this reason, *San Francisco* did not cut her taut wire at Buoy 5 but kept it running until the squadron slowed to take in paravanes, near Cromarty—122 miles of wire run out, without a break.

The succeeding excursion was similar, with Rear Admiral L. Clinton-Baker, R. N., in H. M. S. *Princess Margaret,* in command of the whole force, Rear Admiral Strauss again on board *San Francisco.* On the way out, it was not permitted to pass between the Orkneys and the western end of the minefield planted just previously, but instead, the squadrons were routed NW'ly, through Stronsay and Westray Firths, in the Orkneys, thence E'ly through Fair Island Channel, and down to within five miles north of the other minefield.

While standing through Stronsay Firth in a long, single column, the British squadron, which was in the lead, opened fire on its starboard quarter, its escorting destroyers gathering to drop bombs about a certain spot. Upon signal from the *Princess Margaret,* the starboard wing destroyers of our escort speeded ahead to join the attack, but the port wing destroyers remained on station, although the leading squadron's destroyers had left theirs. In a few moments, a submarine broached about 1500 yards, two points on *San Francisco's* starboard bow, heading across to port, through the column, between the two squadrons. Some destroyers followed and continued bombing. Smoke screens were laid by our escort (*Vampire,* Captain Godfrey, and 11 others of 14th Flotilla) and by our own ships, which thus had a good test for their smoke outfits. *Roanoke* chanced to have a steering engine disablement just at this moment, causing her to sheer out and shift to hand gear, and the *Housatonic* also had some steering trouble, but there was no mishap, and the submarine also for the time escaped. By good luck, an official photographer happened to be on board *San Francisco,* and he got some pictures of genuine activity.

A delay at the morning rendezvous, the long distance round about, and adverse current combined to make a late mining start. While the mining was in progress, the bodies of two German sailors were passed, and a heavy explosion was observed in the eighth minefield, five miles distant, in a position that plotted in the same place a submarine would be which had been reported shortly before.

Darkness shut in about an hour before planting was completed but it caused no suspension nor interference. At the end of the field, buoys were dropped as usual, and all ships together turned left, without signal but on orders given before dark, to the course north, then formed in two columns for the run home. The British and American squadrons had now separated and they passed back through Westray Firth in succession after daylight next morning. Off Pentland Skerries a suspicious craft ahead caused another submarine alarm, and the escort again enveloped the squadron in a smoke screen, but the alarm proved false.

This time, the 10 American vessels had planted six lines, two at each of the usual levels, 46 miles long, 5520 mines in all, the maximum of any excursion; the 4 British vessels planted one line at deep level, 1300 mines, 32 miles long, making altogether 6820 mines on the excursion, the largest single minefield ever planted—done in 3 hours and 50 minutes. Upon returning to the bases, Admiral Strauss signaled "The Commander Mine Force congratulates the squadron on this biggest and most successful excursion."

CHAPTER FIFTEEN
FINISHING THE BARRIER

The conference at Malta at which Rear Admiral Strauss was the American representative recommended extensive mine barrages in the Mediterranean, in locations where the depths of water were much greater than any yet mined, involving winter operations for us. As a first step, Captain Murfin was sent down to Bizerta, near Tunis, to establish a base there, like his two in Scotland—though under much less favorable conditions. Considerable experimenting at home was likewise involved, to develop a suitable extra-deep mine and its moorings. Experienced personnel being needed for this, orders came placing the *Baltimore* at disposition of our Naval Bureau of Ordnance for the purpose. Accordingly, on the tenth excursion, 26 September, she parted company off Scapa Flow, sailing thence two days later for home. In the nine other ships, 97 per cent of the mine capacity remained, but as an experienced vessel of regular man-of-war type, the *Baltimore's* value in the squadron had far exceeded her proportionate capacity.

The minelaying squadrons were now doubling and trebling the barrage, which had been carried clear across the North Sea on the eighth excursion, 7 September. Hitherto we had been favored by good weather, but the season of frequent storms was approaching and already the lengthening hours of darkness made a considerable difference.

Our one loss of life at sea occurred just as the *Baltimore* left us. The *Saranac's* port paravane was running badly and, in clearing it, George C. Anderson, chief boatswain's mate, stepped out on the davit—a sudden jerk! and he was gone. Although search was made, he was never seen again. He had been an energetic yet safe leader, never allowing another man to go overside without a bowline around him, but of himself had been less careful.

An almost unbroken record of ten excursions carried through without breakdown or delay made such a performance now seem a matter of course. The artificer personnel of all ships made a fine showing in upkeep and in steady steaming at sea, notwithstanding that overhaul time was very limited. On returning to port, the squadron would prepare immediately for another excursion and would then wait from day to day for the escort, under notice too short for the extensive overhaul desirable. As the operation progressed, making more wear and tear, the intervals between excursions became shorter and bad weather frequently necessitated keeping steam ready, in case the anchors dragged, as often they did, all which reduced the repair time. Unfinished details of conversion, hard usage in former hands, absence of spare feed pumps and similar secondary dependencies, and a large amount of auxiliary machinery for the vessels' size,—all these were work-making factors. Yet, except for wear, the general condition of all machinery steadily improved.

A large amount of self-repair was done, the *Roanoke* being almost wholly self-sustaining, resorting very little even to our own repair ship *Black Hawk*. The *San Francisco's* carpenter gang built an excellent emergency cabin under the bridge in about 10 days. Then the *Shawmut* and *Aroostook* by themselves increased their oil fuel capacity by 50 per cent, which later enabled them to make the run homeward unassisted and unescorted.

Procedure in conducting the squadron aimed at steadiness in steaming and steering. No unnecessary chances were taken, but neither was the treatment tender. The ships always worked near their speed limit, with only the reserve needed for tactical reasons. Their good performance was due to careful, intelligent foresight, and the rarity of even minor disablements is proof of noteworthy ability and fidelity on the part of the engine and fireroom personnel. No ship was ever late, no minelaying operation ever interrupted, only one hot bearing occurred, only once did a ship's engine have to stop—for but a few minutes—in 8400 miles steaming.

As for steady station-keeping, some ships, notably *Canandaigua,* were always there—hour after hour, night and day—and the others were seldom out. Approaching and during the minelaying, they were very accurate. As one visiting officer from the fleet said, "You've got it on the battleships," and it was officially reported by Admiral Mayo that

The minelayers, though of diverse types, maneuvered well together and kept station very well indeed; they appeared to be under excellent control, both individually and as units, at all times. The laying operation which was witnessed was carried out according to plan without hitch of any kind, thus indicating the efficacy of the preparation, including planning, and the thorough understanding of the work by all concerned.

Much official interest was taken in our operation and brief visits to the bases and the ships were made during the summer by Vice Admiral Sims, Admiral Sir Rosslyn Wemyss, the British First Sea Lord, Vice Admiral Ommaney of the Admiralty, Rear Admiral Clinton-Baker, R. N., the House of Representatives' Naval Committee, and Assistant Secretary Franklin D. Roosevelt. Several of our naval officers went out on excursions, and Lieut. Commander DeSalis, R. N., always a welcome, enthusiastic supporter, went on several of them. They all admired the orderly, complete, and ample arrangements of the mine assembling bases and were especially complimentary about the new minelayers.

Officers and men felt intense pride in their ships, and spared no effort to keep them in regular man-of-war condition. The ten made a handsome squadron, and in capacity for carrying mines, in equipment for handling and planting them continuously, and general arrangement and quality, the new American minelayers were admittedly superior to any others.

Their capacity and performance was the subject of much favorable comment and careful study by the British Admiralty. Besides large mine capacity, their mine elevators were a striking feature. The very first thing considered in the plans had been how to get the lower deck mines up to the launching deck, so that a ship's entire load might be planted in one unbroken string. The Otis Elevator Company's representatives had been called in at the outset and, after several alternatives had been examined, their standard platform type was decided upon, each elevator lifting two mines every 20 seconds. Six elevators in the four largest ships, four in two others, were in use 9 months in all kinds of weather at sea. Only one of the 32 elevators ever failed, and that one just once!

The British minelayers had had trouble from the mine tracks opening and closing with the working of the ship in a seaway. In ours, the tracks were secured to steel crossties mounted on wooden bolsters, the strength and stiffness of the tie, with the elasticity of the bolster, keeping the rails true to gauge, notwithstanding they were lighter rails than the British used. Special interest was taken also in the simple, light switches used in our ships' mine tracks. Some of the Admiralty officials were hard to convince that these switches actually worked, even when operated before their eyes.

While the ships were embarking mines and coaling for the twelfth excursion, Admiral H. T. Mayo, Commander-in-Chief, Atlantic Fleet, accompanied by Captain O. P. Jackson, his Chief of Staff, Rear Admiral Strauss, and Captain N. C. Twining, Chief of Staff to Vice Admiral Sims, made an informal ship inspection, after which Rear Admiral Strauss published the following:

8 October, 1918.

Admiral Mayo, commander-in-chief, left the headquarters of the mine force yesterday evening for the south.

He expressed himself as highly pleased with the zeal, loyal cooperation and efficiency of the mine force both ashore and afloat and congratulated us on the work we have accomplished.

The commander of the mine force is unable to give any data as to the number of enemy submarines that have been destroyed as a result of our efforts, but it is practically certain that the toll is considerable.

The commander-in-chief emphasized the part that the mine force is taking against the enemy as a distinct military offensive, thoroughly known and appreciated at home.

Admiral Mayo found things in their normal condition, with no preparation made for him, as some ships were coaling, others embarking mines. He was evidently pleased with all that he saw, and he remarked how fortunate it was that we had been training in that kind of work, in the old, small mine force, for two years past.

Bad weather during some part of an excursion became now the rule. Coming through a narrow passage in Westray Firth one morning, strong tide against a strong wind made an ugly cross sea, knocking us down to eight knots. One destroyer broached to, and for a few moments lay between our columns, wallowing heavily, as if the next roll would surely take her under.

Shortly afterwards, one arm of the *Quinnebaug's* rudder quadrant broke, and the other arm bent almost to the point of fracture. Had it too gone, she could not have escaped wreck on the rocky channel side. Fortunately she was able to gain partial shelter; in two hours she made repairs and, taking after the rest at top speed, she arrived at Invergordon only 45 minutes behind them. As a coastwise merchant liner, she was often behind time, but in naval hands she developed speed to spare, frequently maintaining on natural draft 10 per cent more than her former best speed under forced draft.

Passing mines adrift was a frequent occurrence. Occasionally we would have to turn out for them. If of the moored type originally, broken away from their anchors, they should be safe when drifting. But of course safety devices, like all others, not infrequently fail to function, especially after immersion in sea water. We let the mines alone, but occasionally an escort destroyer would fire a few rounds, to sink them.

A German floating mine, upon one occasion, was sighted nearly ahead by the *Quinnebaug,* at a moment when her port paravane, running foul, had been hauled in, to clear it. Thrown overboard bodily, the paravane fell on its back, and fortunately righting itself, came in contact with the floating mine, which apparently had a mooring line attached to it, and towed it along with the ship for probably 30 seconds—when the mine detached itself and floated astern. While this was going on on deck, a fire broke out below, in the midst of the mines on the stowage deck. The ship's cooks, who were in the galley at work, with the greatest promptness seized hand fire extinguishers, climbed over between the mines and extinguished the flames. The *Quinnebaug* started planting within two minutes after this danger was averted.

How such a fire would have spread in one of these ships, so full of woodwork, was shown on board the sister ship, *Saranac,* after our return, in January, 1919, at Hampton Roads. The very night after discharging her mines a fire broke out, spreading with such rapidity that the sleeping officers had to escape in their night clothes, losing all their effects, and the men in the engine room were barely able to attend the pumps without suffocation.

The longest single minefield on record was the twelfth, laid on 13 October,—first an $8\frac{1}{2}$ mile stretch 5 lines wide, then 65 miles 3 lines wide, $73\frac{1}{2}$ miles in all. It was begun at 7.33 a. m. and finished at 2.52, over 7 hours. In the latter part, we ran closer than usual to the adjacent field, to keep inside the proclaimed barrage limits. That night, steaming at easy speed so as not to make the entrance to Westray Firth before daylight, radio orders were received from the Commander-in-Chief, Grand Fleet, about 11 o'clock, to proceed with despatch into Westray Firth. Other messages were intercepted, indicating that enemy vessels were out, and as we passed Pentland Skerries next forenoon an unusually large number of British destroyers and sweepers and an observation balloon were searching that vicinity for mines and submarines. Quiet was returning, after a night of greater activity than for a long time.

CHAPTER SIXTEEN

The Thirteenth Excursion

The thirteenth minefield was to be partly in Area A, extending from its southeast corner across Area C towards Udsire Island, ending at a point three miles short of a minefield which the Norwegians had planted around Udsire. All mines were of the upper level, and, as the depth varied from 70 to 150 fathoms, three kinds of anchors were used, which necessitated special care as to the order in which mines were stowed in the ships. The purpose of this field was to close the gap between the British and American minefields in Area C, and the American minefields in Area A, and also to increase the surface obstruction across Area C by two more lines of upper level mines.

No duty could surpass this series of mining excursions for interest sustained to the end. The few events and noteworthy features so far mentioned may perhaps seem to conflict with this statement, but the smoothness of operation constantly striven for tended to eliminate interior incidents, and no mere description can ever impart an adequate impression of our experiences. Keen anticipation, attention ever alert, and a sense of adventure were fresh on each occasion. There was sameness enough in the occupations while in port—coaling, cleaning, embarking mines, and liberty in small towns, but life underway meant something doing all the time which every one felt worth while. Until back at the buoy again, inward bound, it was all activity, the hours often crowded, the whole period sleepless for those in command, never dull for any one. Only as the anchors went down and the tension relaxed could one realize how fast we were living. To quote a *Saranac* poet—

> "They gave us a job we had to do,
> A little bit risky—yes—that's true;
> A good deal like work, both night and day
> But a darn good game for a man to play."

From the earliest discussion of the Northern Barrage project, one of its probable developments was, by general acceptance, to draw out the German fleet, and that ever present possibility gave an added spice to the work. Someone characterized our operations as " An important military offensive with a front seat at the second battle of Jutland," and at the time of the thirteenth excursion it seemed as if the mine squadron might indeed be the bait. Due to the prospect of the German fleet coming out, the squadron was ready a full week before Admiral Beatty could spare a destroyer escort for us.

The *San Francisco* and six other planters made this excursion, the *Roanoke* and *Canandaigua* being omitted. They had been docking at Newcastle-on-Tyne when the mine embarking was done, and although they returned in time to have joined without altering the loading of the other ships, other considerations, external to our Force, determined that they should not go. With *Vampire,* Captain Godfrey, as escort leader for the tenth time, departure was made from Cromarty buoy at 1.30 p. m., Thursday, 24 October. An earlier departure had been first ordered, but a message from the Grand Fleet held us back a few hours.

A storm warning was out as we sailed, and that night the storm overtook us, continuing with varying intensity all the next day and night. Friday forenoon, H. M. S. *Primrose* pointed out and verified Buoy No. 3, and a lull in the storm gave hope that the mining might be carried out that day; but the wind freshened again before the starting point was reached. The ships rolled deeply with their heavy loads, from 27 to 32 degrees each way, but suffered no damage, and the mine installations stood the severe test very well. Through Friday night the squadron cruised back and forth 15 miles either side of the buoy, as far as adjacent minefields would permit. We could not afford to go far away from the buoy, as the time within which we must complete the task was limited and was now scant. After the first turn about, the destroyers disappeared in the darkness, and it was a relief to feel that at least they were clear of possible collision. We needed no screen in such weather and could dispense with them for the night. In the morning they were back again, the weather moderated, *Vampire* pointed out the buoy, and we could proceed.

Mining began at 1.27 p. m. and continued according to schedule until two hours after sunset. The sea and swell had died out so quickly that conditions were very good for mining. All went smoothly; 3760 mines were planted, the last 37 miles being over water up to 150 fathoms deep. As the first four vessels completed their strings, they were ordered to cross ahead of the remaining planting vessels and take station on the southern wing, off *San Francisco's* starboard quarter, where they would be clear of the British minefield which lay just to the north of us. Three destroyers with high-speed minesweeps out preceded the line of planting vessels until an hour after dark, 5.30 p. m. They then joined the other destroyers to starboard and southward of us. In darkness, and in silence except for the mine detonations astern from time to time, the *San Francisco, Canonicus,* and *Housatonic,* in line abreast, stood on a half-hour longer, to the end of the mining track, with no vessels to sweep or to screen ahead as we drew near the coast. The coastal mountains of Norway and a searchlight playing on the clouds were sighted at considerable distance, but not distinctly enough at any time to make an identified bearing. Udsire Island was dimly sighted in the direction expected, but it was too dark to obtain a definite fix, as its light was not burning. On our left was a field of British mines, eight miles away by the chart, but of uncertain distance in fact, since storms and the coastal current might have moved some of the mines in the ten weeks since they were planted, or broken some adrift. The ships kept on to within three miles, by the chart, of the Norwegian minefield ahead—presumably in place and the mines presumably safe if broken adrift. One lacks, however, the same confidence in other people's mines and minefields as in one's own, and more than the usual relief was felt when our schedule was finished.

Then, promptly, all ships and destroyers turned right 90 degrees, again turning right, five minutes later, 70 degrees more, to course W. by S. The squadron then formed in two columns and, when seven miles clear of the minefield, ran parallel to it on the reverse of the mining course, for observation. A curious effect was experienced here, the first occasion where we were heading generally toward a freshly laid field, instead of directly away. The vessel's movement through the water towards the mines enhanced the sharpness of shock from the exploding defective ones—to such an extent that both officers and men came on the bridge in real concern, reporting that we must have struck something.

It was noteworthy during this thirteenth excursion that the management of the ships, always good before, continued so, in spite of the heavy weather. About 9.00 p. m. following a hard squall which came in the midst of a turn, causing the ships to get considerably out of station, three successive 90-degree turns were made and the squadron was then formed, upon signal, in a new order, for more convenience during the rest of the night. All was done in good time, yet without any vessels coming uncomfortably near in the course of it. Next day, the last two hours of mining were after sunset, but no lights were shown nor tactical signal made. All maneuvers at the finish were made at prescribed clock times, in obedience to signals sent before dark.

The supporting force sighted us about 1.55 p. m. Friday, 12 miles off, then stood to the westward. About 9.30 a. m. Saturday a light cruiser of the support communicated and at 2.00 p. m. the whole support was sighted again, to the southward, consisting of the second battle cruiser squadron, the fifth battle squadron, and the seventh light cruiser squadron. Vice Admiral Pakenham, in H. M. S. *Lion,* commanding the Battle Cruiser Force, was in command of the whole. This excursion took our squadron farther afield than it had been since June. After the third excursion, all our planting had been done behind a barrier of our own making or else close to British waters, but on this occasion we were on the exposed side of the whole barrage.

Late Sunday night, 27 October, the squadron returned to port, and by the following Wednesday, 30 October, all nine ships were again loaded, and there they waited, for 12 days of vile weather, ready for another excursion. The one planned would have completed the fourth system, extending northeasterly from the end of the twelfth minefield. But no more mining was necessary, and upon the signing of the armistice, the mines on the launching decks were disembarked from the ships, to give more space for the crews. Preparations were then taken up for returning to the United States.

Of six months in European waters to the date of the armistice, on 33 days the squadron or some of its ships were underway, steaming in the North Sea more than 8400 miles. So far as readiness of the squadron was concerned, the excursions could have been made with greater rapidity—never was an excursion delayed on account of a ship's not being prepared. During the five months of minelaying activity, the intervals between excursions averaged 10 days. The time actually consumed in embarking mines, coaling, and routine overhaul came to less than four days, so that four excursions a month could have been made, but for the delays incident to manufacture and to considerations external to our Force.

CHAPTER SEVENTEEN

RESULTS

Altogether there were 13 regular excursions and two special ones by the American squadron, and 11 by the British squadron. In all, 70,117 mines were planted, of which 56,571, or four-fifths, were American. In its 230 miles length, the barrage varied in width from 15 to 35 miles, so that a submarine could not attempt a crossing without being in danger for from one to three hours, or twice as long, if running submerged. The obstruction extended to a depth of 240 feet, except over the eastern section of 50 miles length, where the deepest mines were submerged 125 feet.

In small fields, of a few score or hundreds of mines, laid piecemeal by fixed marks, the mines in adjacent lines are usually " staggered," so as to halve and block the opposite intervals, but in an open-sea minefield of immense area, far beyond sight of any marks and laid at 12 knots speed or faster, no such nicety is possible or necessary. The great Northern Barrage opposed from 6 to 10 lines of mines to a submarine on the surface and three to four lines more at whatever depth the submarine might think he could safely pass. Absolute impassability never was attained nor expected. At the thickest part a submarine had one chance in ten of getting through. The explosion of defective mines had left some thin spots—but who could tell where? Such a minefield is not so much like a Chinese wall as it is like a stretch of rough, treacherous country, whose crossing would always be a desperate venture.

Submarines are known to have crossed the barrier, but they all feared it, and as early as 8 July, 1918, some experienced its deadly effect. From the very circumstances of the barrier's great extent and the absence of observers, the full toll, in damage as well as destruction, may never be known. The official statistics of lost German submarines, compiled March 1, 1919, credit the Northern Barrage with the destruction of four submarines certainly, two more probably, and possibly still two more. An equal number were severely damaged, though not destroyed, and it is considered probable by the British Admiralty that the loss of five other submarines, the cause of which cannot be definitely proven, is accounted for by the Northern Barrage. Thus by reliable records, the toll was 17. Indications during the sweeping up of the barrage tend to confirm this. Besides these, to the squadron's credit, should be added the two submarines reported lost in the North Irish Channel, in the field which consisted of British mines laid by our *Baltimore*.

The summary of Activities of U. S. Naval Forces in European Waters, issued by Admiral Sims, says further:

There is no doubt that this barrage had a considerable moral effect on the German naval crews, for it is known that several submarines hesitated some time before crossing. Also, reports from German sources are that the barrage caused no small amount of panic in some of the submarine flotillas.

It is also probable that the barrage played a part in preventing raids on Allied commerce by fast enemy cruisers.

In thus deterring a sally by enemy cruisers, the barrage aided the mission of the American Battleship Division Six, under Rear Admiral T. S. Rodgers, U. S. N., flagship *Utah,* which was sent over to guard the convoys and was based on Berehaven, Ireland.

One officially reported statement of a German submarine captain said that three submarines, including his own, had been damaged by the barrage but all had reached port. The injury in his case prevented his diving. Other accounts, in the press and from individuals, give some indication of the moral effect produced by this great mine-field, reaching to the German Army and also among civilians.

It would be interesting to know what proportion of the submarines that passed the line of the barrier were harmed by it, but the effect upon the enemy went far beyond such tangible injuries. Every successive case of being damaged yet escaping destruction would increase the moral effect, and magnify the number of losses that would be attributed to the barrage, as other submarines failed to return. Official summaries rate depth charges first, mines next, in importance among the five most effective measures against submarines.

A mark of royal approval was indirectly conferred upon the Mine Force undertaking after only one excursion, in the bestowal upon Rear Admiral Strauss of the honor Knight Commander of St. Michael and St. George, and our operations received mention later by the First Sea Lord of the British Admiralty in his reply to the congratulatory message of Admiral Sims upon the conclusion of the armistice:

We recognize with a feeling of gratitude the debt we owe to the United States Navy for its wholehearted support during the past 18 months, not only in the submarine campaign and extensive minelaying programme, but also in sending the Atlantic squadron to reinforce the Grand Fleet . . .

During the four months intervening, the press made occasional brief reference to the effectiveness of the North Sea barrier but, compared to other operations, ours received scant mention. A veil of general silence was deemed necessary for our doings, and the policy of concealing the destruction of submarines stood in the way of even telling our men the few authentic reports we did receive of damage to the enemy from our own work.

One account, widely copied in the British and home press, described the barrier, which we had begun and were still at work upon, as already a fact and a British accomplishment! And when, in October, the story was released in America, the accounts which reached us dwelt mainly upon the parts of the work done on shore. As the Secretary of the Navy put it, the minelaying was done with " no glamour nor romance nor appreciation."

It was not in the character of our officers and men, however, to feel discontent. Thoroughly interested in their work and convinced of its importance, they were satisfied to have it progressing well, and to wait for their part to receive its due.

Admiral Sims expressed his recognition shortly before we sailed from Portland, England, for home. All the commanding officers, many other officers, and 25 men from each minelayer were assembled on board the *San Francisco,* and when the admiral came on board, his flag was broken at the main truck. After brief mention of the large numbers and the many activities of our naval forces in European waters, he said that the Mine Force—

had done a stunt the like of which had not been done in the world before. After we came into the war we designed a mine, built it, equipped the minelayers, sent them over to this side and planted more mines in less space of time than any nation in the world ever thought of doing before. As to the efficiency of the mine barrier, that is something that has not concerned you so particularly as those who designed it; but fitting out the vessels, learning to handle the mines, planting them, and going through the strenuous work has been really one of the finest accomplishments of the navy on this side. . . . . as a nautical feat, a piece of seamanship, it has been perfectly successful.

Another thing particularly gratifying is that the conduct of the men of the Mine Force at their bases and at sea has been exemplary. I think one thing that has impressed itself on this side more than any other is the conduct of our men. They were inclined to regard us, when we first came over here, as men out of the wilds of America. I think they rather wanted to strengthen their police force when we came around. They found out it was not necessary. Not only have you created a good impression by your conduct as far as seamanship is concerned, but you have created a splendid impression socially. We hear it on all sides. . . . .

I wish you a Merry Christmas and a Happy New Year; and when you get back there you can tell them all about it. You need not feel that you have to tell them you did the whole thing. Just tell them a straight story and you may be more than satisfied with that. . . . .

The Secretary of the Navy's annual report characterizes the Northern Barrage as "the outstanding anti-submarine offensive project of the year," and elsewhere he wrote of it as "a truly wonderful work," the story of it "one of the thrilling contributions of what the navy men did in the war."

Admiral Benson, Chief of Naval Operations, our highest professional authority, considered the achievement of the Mine Force one of the most successful efforts of the whole war by any of the forces engaged. Not only has the North Sea barrage had a deterring effect necessarily on the enemy, but it has convinced the European nations that there is no task which the United States once undertakes to perform that they cannot and will not successfully carry through. I believe that the moral effect alone of the North Sea barrage, not only on the enemy, but on our friends, to say nothing of the excellent training to our own personnel, will be worth more to the country than all the money and time spent upon it.

Actual serious damage to submarines, in amount comparing well with that done by patrol and escort vessels in thrice the period of time, panic among submarine flotillas, probable deterrence of cruiser raids, and considerable moral effect at home and abroad—these results were well worth while. And is it not more than probable that the barrage weighed heavily towards the German collapse? Imperfect though it was—expected to be so in its first consideration—still, there it stood, a deadly menace already, which could and would become more and more effective, the more the submarine campaign was persisted in. That campaign could not hope to survive it.

CHAPTER EIGHTEEN

GENERAL LIVING CONDITIONS

No account of the mining excursions would be complete without some description of the conditions in which the ships' companies worked. The accommodations on board were sufficient for their officers and, when clear of mines and the weather such as to permit hatches and air ports to be open, the crew's quarters were roomy and comfortable. Upon embarking mines, however, the crew spaces in all ships except *Shawmut* and *Aroostook* became very cramped, and as the season advanced, mines were on board during a greater part of the time, while rainy weather became more frequent, thus making more discomfort on board with less diversion on shore. The simplest movement below decks was interfered with by the mines; moreover, their presence forbade moving pictures on board, restricted smoking, and limited the " happy hours " and similar forms of diversion, so common in our navy and so particularly desirable in our circumstances.

After the third excursion it became the rule to embark the mines as soon as possible after returning to base. For the one night following a planting, the ships' decks would be clear for hammocks, and all the watch below might then swing on their billets. Occasionally there would be one more night before the mines would be in the way again, but generally most of the ships would begin to take coal or mines on the day following their return to port. Thus the period of rest allowed, after the physical exertion and the tension of a mining excursion, was brief.

Ventilation was always poor at sea, especially in the *Roanoke* and *Quinnebaug* classes. The intended ventilation systems had not been completed, no ship having more than 60 per cent of the designed supply of air and some less than 40 per cent. On the lower mine decks, with steam on the elevator pumps and mine winches, and considerable numbers of men in the track crews, the air became very close, foul, and hot. As the weather grew bad, causing seasickness below, the condition of the lower decks and the air may be imagined, making an extensive cleaning and airing out imperative immediately on reaching port.

All the ships' crews numbered considerably more than originally intended, because extra men were found to be needed and still others were taken, in training for the general naval supply. Notwithstanding the crowding and other unfavorable conditions, partial inspections in the course of the summer and thorough inspections at the close showed that in upkeep and cleanliness—as well as in mining, steaming, signaling, tactical handling, boating, messing, and discipline—the state of affairs in all departments was highly creditable to any type of ship.

The crowded conditions on board, the lack of deck space, and the tense and arduous character of the men's normal work, made diversion on shore more than ordinarily necessary. Thanks to the energy and tact of Commander Canaga and the squadron athletic officer, Lieut. Commander Hewlett, and to the co-operation of the ships' athletic officers, interest in athletics was well sustained, a series of well-played baseball games giving entertainment to the townspeople as well as the men, and doing much to promote friendly relations, as described in an earlier chapter. And thanks are due in large measure to the local residents for their hospitality extended to both officers and men. The opening of the Northern Meetings' building, well equipped, by the American Y. M. C. A., and a large reception by Captain and Mrs. Rowley at Inverness, and a similar initiative by Rear Admiral and Mrs. Pears at Invergordon, gave such things a good start, which carried on throughout our stay.

Inverness being headquarters for the relief of prisoners of war in Germany belonging to the Cameron Highlanders, and Invergordon for the Seaforth Highlanders, our people attended the fairs and sports in considerable numbers, bringing in new life and spirit, as well as swelling the receipts. The bands from our two bases and from the *San Francisco* were in constant demand through all the neighboring country, and exhibition games of baseball made another drawing feature. After the Black Isle fête, at the ancient little town of Fortrose, the manager wrote that the *San Francisco's* band had brought in £27 from the sale of programs alone, and the whole intake was more than double the previous year's.

For the Cameron Highlanders' sports, the Countess of Elgin organized a toy-making competition, offering souvenir prizes. Our men entered into the idea with more interest than expected, producing many articles of real value, none that did not bring a good price, and helping materially to make the toy stall a great success. Before sailing for home, the men afloat and ashore combined in presenting a fund exceeding $500 to equip a new school playground for the Inverness boys and girls.

When the summer had passed and darkness came on early, dances became frequent, the Scottish lassies quickly learning the American steps. The erstwhile quiet little Queensgate hotel did a rushing business, its ball room being taken, by sailors or officers, six nights in the week. And the men of Base 18, together with amateur talent of Inverness, staged a show, of which Admiral Sims, who saw it in London, said:

I saw your show, the second part of it, in London the other day. It had anything of its kind I have seen skinned to death. There isn't another one that holds a candle to it. It is particularly gratifying that the show included a number of the young girls of Inverness. The show was clean and refined and splendid in every way. It was a pleasure to go behind the curtain and thank them and to kiss that wee bit of a girl who used to do the dance.

These diversions kept the men in good spirits and up to the mark in their work. They were the more useful because of our comparative isolation and concealment. The best was made of whatever came, with unabated zeal, steady improvement, and cheerfulness always. Despite the high prices of clothing and the excessive wear and tear on uniforms from the mines, the crews kept themselves, as well as their ships, in creditable appearance. Their discipline was excellent, their behavior on shore on all occasions repeatedly evoking favorable comment, both official and private, and their fine spirit showed also in a handsome subscription to the Liberty Loans, the squadron taking of the fourth loan five dollars for each mine in their fields. As a visiting naval officer reported:

The whole Mine Force is short on criticism and complaints, but long on work and results, and the navy should be intensely proud of them.

CHAPTER NINETEEN

FAREWELL TO THE HIGHLANDS

The squadron's task was not finished with the signing of the armistice, for some of the unused mines had to be carried back. Two weeks passed before orders came for home—all kinds of rumors were rife meanwhile, and the wait was the more trying because of the influenza quarantine against amusement resorts. This had its benefit, in that the Mine Force escaped the epidemic almost entirely, but with the season too far advanced and rainy for athletics and the Y. M. C. A. closed, the quarantine bore hard on the men afloat.

So long as the mines were on board, no relaxation of discipline could be permitted, and in order to keep the men well occupied, infantry and rifle practice were added to the ship drills, and formal inspections of ships were begun. The prospect of these inspections always keys things up. All ships did well, but the last one inspected, *Roanoke,* Captain Stearns, surpassed all expectation, being a model—judged by the highest standard—of efficient organization, training, and administration, pervaded by a uniformly high and loyal spirit.

One great test was to rig for getting the mines out in case of fire—though a forlorn hope at best, since 15 minutes (the time in which the mines would explode when exposed to fire) would scarcely suffice to begin discharging. The promise of Commander Beck, *Roanoke's* executive officer, to be ready in 10 minutes was received by his colleagues with derision. When the test came, he stood quietly by, letting his men work without coaching. A flicker of patient resignation came over his face as he saw that some zealot had disabled one of the winches to be used by putting oil on the friction-clutch, because " it looked like bright work." But in spite of the consequent delay, all was ready in only *six* minutes. " I thought I was some little executive myself," said one colleague, " but I've got nothing more to say."

Fortunately the quarantine was raised in time for full enjoyment of our last week in the Highlands. Our friends omitted nothing in hospitality and goodwill. Entertaining on board had been an extreme rarity during the minelaying, but now it could be permitted, and the squadron had the honor of a visit from The Mackintosh of Mackintosh, chief of Clan Chattan, colonel of the Cameron Highlanders, lord lieutenant of Invernesshire, who had been most hospitable to us. All the captains were assembled on board the *San Francisco* to receive him and afterwards to lunch with him. He inspected the crew and ship with Captain Butler, his first visit to an American man-of-war since 1870 in Gibraltar, on board the old *Kearsarge*. Chancing to ask a man's name, the reply " Scott, sir," made everything after that go smoothly.

On our national Thanksgiving Day, Rear Admiral Clinton-Baker sent a message to Rear Admiral Strauss, which, with the latter's reply, expressed cordial satisfaction in working together and in the mutual regard and respect sprung up, which would help to bring the two great navies into still closer union. A theater party and reception at Invergordon and a formal dinner and ball at Inverness were given that day by British naval officers. The ball was held in the " Northern Meeting " rooms, the annual assembly place of all the Highland nobility and gentry. This was the first dance there since the war began, and it was a most enjoyable affair, picturesque with dress kilts and lively with the Highland fling. Next day the enlisted men were given a ball in the same place, which usually held 700, but on this occasion 1400. Next morning my orderly, Rose, could not wait for me to appear but woke me up to hear, " Commodore, the British treated us *fine!* "

On Saturday, the American officers gave a return ball, which was as well attended as we could desire, and so, at midnight, festivities ended.

Our sailing being set for Sunday midnight, there could be no gatherings at the actual departure, but just before noon Captain Rowley came out to the *San Francisco* with Mrs. Rowley and a small party, to say goodbye, and at Invergordon Rear Admiral Pears went on board the *Roanoke,* to use her radio telephone for his parting message to me. From late that afternoon until midnight the flagship's signal bridge had no respite, farewell messages and replies continuing until we were clear of the harbor. All were the same tenor—appreciation of the work accomplished, " pleasant and friendly memory, goodbye and God speed." The recollections taken away of beautiful country and kindly people could only make us wish to revisit them.

Among the last signals exchanged with the shore were:

To: Commander Mine Squadron One:

The Commander Mine Force wishes to thank the officers and the men of the Mine Squadron for their efficient work and loyal cooperation and wishes them a happy return to the United States.

To: Commander Mine Force:

The Squadron Commander in behalf of the captains, officers, and men of Mine Squadron One returns sincere acknowledgment for the Commander Mine Force. Signal of thanks and good wishes. The Squadron is deeply gratified to receive his approbation for its part in his unprecedented undertaking so successfully accomplished.

CHAPTER TWENTY
SCAPA FLOW

The Mine Force was not represented at the surrender of the German fleet, but on our way to Portland, where leave was to be given before sailing for home, we passed through Scapa Flow to see the surrendered ships.

As our long, single column approached the British squadrons lying at anchor, on guard, a signal invited us to steer between their lines, and as we wound in between the battleships and battle cruisers, their crews were assembled on deck—very striking in solidity of mass and evenness of rank and file. They cheered each passing minelayer, our crews running from side to side to make response, the bands playing the national airs, and signals being exchanged.

To: Admiral First Battle Squadron.
From: Commander Mine Squadron One.

Captain Belknap presents his compliments and regrets that his movement orders do not permit paying his respects in person to Admiral Madden. The U. S. Mine Squadron sends congratulations upon the great success that has brought about this unprecedented spectacle. 0919.

From: Admiral Madden.
To: Captain Belknap.

Thank you for your 0919. I wish the Mining Squadron speedy return home and have much regret in parting with such a splendid force.

Then silence was ordered, as we neared the Germans' anchorage. First came the destroyers, to the left, moored in pairs with a few British destroyers at their head, and then, on the west side of Cava Island, the large ships came into view. Many signs of their downfallen state were evident, and the sight was to me the more impressive from having seen that fleet in its ascendancy. Now, in some ships scarcely a man was to be seen, on others the rails were crowded, officers and men mingling together, to gaze on their untouched bait.

In quiet procession we had nearly passed them all, when the British trawlers on the opposite side, holding the net across Hoy Sound—had been holding it in fair weather and foul, for three long years—seeing our flag and knowing what our work had been, broke out in long and loud blasts of their whistles—having crews too small for an audible cheer. The *San Francisco* responded with the usual three whistle blasts, which the ships following repeated in succession, but one of them blew her siren instead, and that started them all again. For a few moments there was a fearful din, and how this must have struck the British ships, on the other side of Cava, was indicated by the next signals exchanged soon afterwards:

From: Captain Belknap.
To: Admiral Madden.

Many thanks for your kind message. The Mine Squadron has much enjoyed its duty with the Grand Fleet and is much honored by the association.

From: Admiral Madden.
To: Captain Belknap.

Reply.—Thank you. For your hilarious Mining Squadron, a speedy trip home and have much regret in parting with such a brave bunch.

Clearing the island, we passed H. M. S. *Lion,* flagship of Vice Admiral Pakenham, who had commanded the support on our last excursion. The *Lion* was steaming back and forth across the way out, like a sentry on his beat, a ready check on any German ship that might attempt escape.

Replying to my greeting, the *Lion* flashed from Vice Admiral Pakenham:

I greatly regret that only a farewell signal is possible. You take with you not only my personal regards, but the gratitude and admiration of the Battle Cruiser Force and united wishes for a happy return to your country.

As the squadron passed out of the harbor, the garrisons at the entrance turned out and cheered and one of the seaplanes that had patrolled for submarines while the squadron was planting on some of its excursions sailed over and around the *San Francisco,* each time nearer, until he swooped by with a roar and a wave of the hand, so near that his wing tip passed not 20 feet from the bridge.

Three months afterwards came a letter from Vice Admiral Sir William C. Pakenham:

I trust old friends on your side have enjoyed return to their own country, but we miss them much over here. When your Force steamed through Scapa, I thought Providence as well as skill must have been on your side to enable you to pass through a period of such dangerous service, and yet to take all home.

CHAPTER TWENTY-ONE

HOME

Until departure from Scotland, the squadron had been almost free from the influenza epidemic prevailing elsewhere so seriously, but during the ten-day stay at Portland some cases appeared among men returning from leave. Among 427 persons on board the *San Francisco,* there were 113 cases before the disease was finally checked. Enough officers and leading men escaped, however, to warrant sailing for home with only one day's delay, but leaving 40 men in Portland hospital. A few mild cases developed on board the other ships, fortunately with no serious outcome.

On Saturday, 14 December, the *Shawmut* and *Aroostook* sailed for the Azores, en route for Bermuda and Hampton Roads, their limited fuel radius making these stops necessary. The rest of the squadron followed on Tuesday, 17 December, taking the direct route. The rule of no homeward-bound pennants for less than two years' absence being relaxed on account of exceptional conditions, all ships on leaving Portland flew long streamers—one so long and large from the *Roanoke,* a steam winch was needed to hoist it.

Immediately encountering bad weather, for three days less than half the desired progress was made, and the *San Francisco* had a serious breakdown of her steering gear. Several men were injured while steering by hand, which had to be discontinued, because the sea drove so heavily on the rudder. The ship was then steered by the screws alone for four days until temporary repairs could be made. Upon the weather clearing, it was decided to divide the squadron, allowing *Roanoke, Canandaigua, Housatonic,* and *Quinnebaug* to continue the direct run, which their remaining coal and daily consumption warranted doing, while the *San Francisco, Canonicus,* and *Saranac,* with shorter fuel supply and larger consumption, proceeded by the Azores.

Like other forces coming home, we wished to come into New York, for a touch of the limelight after being so long in obscurity, and because the location was central for letting the men go home. With mines on board, we could not expect a welcome anywhere, and at New York bare permission was doubtful—especially so soon after the Perth Amboy explosions. With no prospect of being *invited* there, we sailed with destination announced as New York as the one possible chance of getting there, but orders soon came to steer for Hampton Roads instead.

Near mid-passage on Christmas night, after dinner, a British collier collided with the *Roanoke,* opening a good-sized hole in her port side forward. Supports of the bridge being knocked away, its end sloped down, making it seem at first that the ship was rapidly settling. Steam from a broken pipe came forth in volumes, to which the red glow of the port sidelight lent the appearance of smoke and flames. Collision and fire, with 500 mines on board, far at sea in cold, misty weather, would have been indeed serious. It needed just that to round out our experiences, but fortune was with us, and the situation was promptly brought under control.

The *Quinnebaug* saw the collier safe into Halifax, and then overtook the other three, all four minelayers arriving at Hampton Roads without further incident on 30 December. The *Shawmut* and *Aroostook* had already come in on the 27th. The rest, pursued by bad weather 10 days out of 16, both Christmas and New Year spent at sea, and feeling our way into port through fog, the *San Francisco* and the two with her arrived early January 3, 1919, making the squadron once more complete, except for the *Baltimore,* still absent on experimenting duty.

In due course, the last mine was safely discharged from our ships, making a clear record of over 60,000 mines handled without mishap. And yet we were not to disperse without one more experience—a serious fire. The very night after the *Saranac* had landed her mines, a fire broke out in the wardroom, spreading so rapidly that, until outside help came, it seemed impossible to prevent her being completely gutted. Only great exertions saved her and the incident showed that our strict guard against fire had been no idle precaution.

7

CHAPTER TWENTY-TWO
THE MINE SWEEPERS

With the removal of the mines in peace, the sweepers came into prominence, which gives occasion to mention an inconspicuous part of the Mine Force work, too easily overlooked. There were four large seagoing tugs in the mine squadron, *Patuxent,* Lieutenant J. B. Hupp; *Patapsco,* Lieutenant W. E. Benson; *Sonoma,* Lieutenant J. S. Thayer; and *Ontario,* Lieutenant E. J. Delavy. These, as fleet tenders had towed targets, carried passengers, mail, stores, and the like. All this continued after they were assigned to the original Mine Force, yet, by a more systematic apportionment of their former duties, time was gained for training in mining and sweeping, enough to arouse a keen interest and foster the Mine Force spirit. In the fleet's tactical and strategical exercises the tugs took part, and upon our entering the war, the antisubmarine net tasks and the experimenting that were assigned to the Mine Force were possible of accomplishment only by the use of these tugs, together with our mine carrier vessel, the *Lebanon,* Lieutenant H. N. Huxford. In seaworthiness, power, and equipment, these vessels had what was needed, but their chief value lay in the resourcefulness and energy of their personnel. Lieutenant E. S. R. Brandt, U. S. N., was their division leader, commanding the *Sonoma,* during their first 18 months in the Mine Force.

Night and day, they were always ready, and it seemed as if their power and seaworthiness would take them anywhere. Well equipped for salvaging, they played an important part in saving the U. S. S. *Olympia* and afterwards the *Texas,* when they grounded, in 1917. Often they had long hours of hard duty, but could always be counted on. Service in them gave excellent experience for both officers and men, and many were the capable petty officers turned out. The question " Can you do it? " was never asked, nor " Are you ready? " It was necessary only to say go and do, and whether foggy or clear, the tug that was sent would nose her way through somehow.

These tugs were not properly equipped for mine sweeping, lacking the special type of winch needed for that purpose, but their 18 months' experience with improvised arrangements yielded information of great value for the new design of a combined sea-going tug and mine-sweeper type, of the *Bird* Class, contracted for during the summer of 1917. By the original plan for the Northern Mine Barrage, the first 12 to be completed of these new sweeping vessels were assigned to the mine squadron, and continued efforts were made to expedite their completion, but without success so far as concerned their joining the mine squadron.

Meantime, in the experiments and tests of the mine, in training the new personnel, and in every kind of transportation and other assistance to the new minelayers during the month preparatory to sailing, the four original tugs were invaluable. The new sweepers not being ready, the original four were fitted out to take part in the work abroad. When the mine squadron left Hampton Roads late in April, 1918, the *Patuxtent* and *Patapsco* were temporarily detached, to proceed by way of Bermuda, the Azores, and Brest, escorting a convoy of submarine chasers across. Rear Admiral Wilson, U. S. N., commended them for being the first to deliver such a convoy intact. They finally arrived at Inverness 24 June, 1918, where they were used to inspect and observe mine-fields, to communicate between the detachments of minelayers at the two bases, and to train men.

The larger pair, *Sonoma* and *Ontario,* were retained with the minelayers until their final sailing for abroad. The *Sonoma,* Lieutenant J. S. Trayer, accompanied the squadron on its trip across, making a notable passage for a vessel of her size. Always ready for any duty, up to station, and able to steam at maximum speed at the end of a 3000-mile run, she earned commendation for her captain and her engineer officer, Lieutenant L. W. Knight, U. S. N.

With the *Ontario,* which accompanied a convoy of submarine chasers across, the *Sonoma,* after a brief stay in Scotland, went to Queenstown, where the need for that type was greater than with the Mine Force. In this assignment their rescue of submarine victims was a continuation in greater degree of similar pre-war assistance, in home and Cuban ports, off Hatteras and Cape Maysi, rendered to vessels in distress from collision, breakdown, and fire at sea.

CHAPTER TWENTY-THREE
THE MINE FORCE, OLD AND NEW

Details of preparation have been only briefly touched upon in the preceding chapters, though actually their influence on the success of the operation deserves more prominence. It will not be supposed that the new squadron just grew, or that in the active operations everything just broke fair. On the contrary, success was earned by logical, consistent preparation, extending back over years and by sound organization and execution when the plan was launched. Hard work, development of doctrine, and prospective study, between 1914 and 1917, bore fruit, and, for the navy's credit, the foresight which produced it deserves record along with the achievement itself.

While suitable and adequate material would ever be the first essential in such an operation, the all-important question lay in the personnel afloat. The excellent qualities of the new mine would be of no avail without proper laying of the barrage. Fortunately we already had a minelaying force, small but capable, so that we did not look abroad for instruction.

Prior to 1914, minelaying from a ship underway had received little attention in our navy, but when some early events of the great European war showed what a part mines were likely to play in the future, mining affairs were made the principal duty of Captain G. R. Marvell in the Navy Department, the conversion of two more minelayers was pushed to completion, and mine training was taken up in earnest in the fleet.

The hitherto solitary mine ship *San Francisco* was taken out of the heterogeneous group known as the Auxiliary Division of our fleet, to become the flagship of a separate organization for mining and mine sweeping, which was established on July 10, 1915, while Admiral F. F. Fletcher had the Atlantic fleet.

In the development of this new branch, which was under my command until September, 1917, one truth came out forcibly, that the sustained attention requisite throughout mining operations could only be insured by keeping everything up in man-of-war style. Laying and recovering mines was messy work, and in a ship of a type long obsolete, classed as auxiliary, and using a weapon of stealth barely tolerated, to maintain such a standard was not easy. As Sir Eric Geddes, First Lord of the British Admiralty, said in a speech in New York, " Before the war, mine-laying was considered unpleasant work for a naval man, an occupation like that of rat-catching, and not attractive."

Whatever aversion may have been felt quickly vanished in the growing interest that had been aroused. Besides its own specialty, the new branch joined the fleet's tactical, gunnery, and strategic exercises, these last leading to new activities and to study of the possibilities of mines and of the logical functions of the Mine Force. Both Admiral Fletcher and his successor, Admiral H. T. Mayo, did all in their power to establish the new element firmly as a regular part of the mobile fleet. Their interest and encouragement had immediate effect in confirming the personnel's sense of value, which had been engendered by the variety of their employment, the stimulating results of their efforts, and belief in the power of their weapon.

Experimenting with submarine nets was also taken up, and in our first six months of war, the Mine Force was employed chiefly in planting three nets in Chesapeake Bay, and one each in Long Island Sound and at Newport entrance. Success with the Long Island net, over five miles long, was only achieved after a hard struggle with a five-knot current, which time after time swept the net away or, crushing its buoys, pulled it under and entwined it with tons of kelp.

Such in outline was the scope of Mine Force activities during the 28 months prior to preparing for the North Sea expedition. We had not yet laid any minefields during the war, but as if in practice for the very operation to come, the Force, early in December, 1916, had laid a minefield off the Jersey Coast, below Sandy Hook—200 loaded mines, in three parallel lines laid simultaneously, and all taken up by next day—the press not notified. Various arrangements in connection with the handling and transportation of mines had been planned and actually practiced. For result—when the Northern Barrage project came under consideration, the question of practicability of the operation could be answered yes with confidence, and the subsequent working out of mining installations, organization, and training was guided by reliable data—all from our own experience.

Many-sided experience had produced a well-knit organization of units that were resourceful, self-reliant, and mutually helpful, well trained on sound lines in minelaying, singly and together. Long hours and work in all weathers were a matter of course. Quiet self-confidence was the mark of the Force spirit. And thus, although the original Mine Force was much too small for the great task ahead, its value as a nucleus and leaven for the greatly enlarged mine squadron to be formed could hardly be overstated.

Since the autumn of 1916, the principal Mine Force officers had been myself, as Force Commander, Commander H. V. Butler, commanding the flagship *San Francisco* and senior aid, Commander A. W. Marshall, U. S. S. *Baltimore,* and Commander T. L. Johnson, U. S. S. *Dubuque.* All these were to take part in the North Sea operation and were concerned in its preparation— myself in charge, Butler training the new crews, Marshall experimenting with the new mine, which Butler concluded, and Johnson helping to select the new ships, then going abroad for information. Their experience and their ships were invaluable both in preparation and afterwards. On the principle that, let material be old or new, discipline may be the best, the style of these seasoned men-of-war, aiming to match the highest naval standard, was always a strong influence in the squadron.

In October, 1917, with the original order to go ahead, which was accompanied by a word of strong approval, from the President down, the development of plans and co-ordination of all preparations became my principal duty in the Office of Naval Operations. Command of a minelayer and two years at the head of mining affairs in the Atlantic fleet had given me experience that was directly pertinent.

The intention being to lay the barrage as soon as possible, and counting five days as the least time between minelaying operations—coaling, embarking mines, out, laying, and back—the expected manufacturing output of 1000 mines a day demanded a minelaying squadron with capacity of 5000 mines at one time. Towards this, our *San Francisco* and *Baltimore* carried together only 350 mines. The eight new vessels would add 5350, thus providing a good margin, either for the loss of a ship or for speeding up.

No time was to be lost. The demand for ships, ship-yard work, and ship equipment for other purposes was increasing every day.

Within 10 days the Eastern Steamship Corporation's fast passenger liners *Massachusetts* and *Bunker Hill,* running daily between New York and Boston, were purchased outright, becoming the *Shawmut* and *Aroostook.* Within a month the Southern Pacific freight steamers *El Rio, El Dia, El Cid,* and *El Siglo* were taken over, becoming *Roanoke, Housatonic, Canonicus,* and *Canandaigua,* respectively. Carrying 860 mines each they soon became known as the Big Four. The Old Dominion steamers *Hamilton* and *Jefferson,* familiar to passengers between New York and Norfolk, followed by December 6, 1917.

The task of making four freight ships habitable for crews of 400 men, at the same time carrying twice as many mines as any

THE BOSTON-NEW YORK PASSENGER LINER "MASSACHUSETTS."
Before conversion into a minelayer.

other vessel of their size, is not done by a wave of the hand, and as for the four passenger steamers taken, they were gutted like fish—saloons and cabins ripped out—before their conversion could begin. Although plans had to be based upon what could be done within a reasonable time, with material and labor scarce, all features had to conform to the requirements of the mining installations. These were almost entirely new on the scale contemplated, either in our own or any other service. There was little data available of similar installations, except some British mining memoranda and a few belated blueprints. Lieutenant DeSalis, R. N., kindly placed his experience at our disposal, which was a help, but attempts abroad had not made a success of mine elevators—which would form a cardinal feature of our installation—

nor had others gone in for mine-carrying capacity to the extent we contemplated—which was the maximum number consistent with not squeezing the crew intolerably. Hence, little of their information proved applicable to our case. Experience in our own minelayers, however, *San Francisco, Baltimore,* and *Dubuque,* during the past three years, enabled many details to be decided with a confidence that subsequent results confirmed.

That winter of 1917-18 will be long remembered! Material was scarce, transportation congested, labor unsettled, fuel short, weather severe, haste and high prices everywhere. Much delay came from lack of interest among workmen. The campaign of

THE 20-KNOT MINELAYER "SHAWMUT."
Formerly the coastwise passenger liner *Massachusetts.*

addresses by good speakers explaining the need for the ships and the men's own interest in doing their best, did not begin until sometime in February, and then only in a small way. There was insufficient supervision, the contractors were converting vessels to a type for which no model existed, and plans were not forthcoming as fast as wanted, often not in the logical order. Besides delays and losses of material in transportation, one trade in which labor was shortest—shipfitter—was the one on whose work much of the other had to wait.

By constant urging and anticipating probable delays, the work as a whole was kept always progressing, even if at times slowly. The captains to be, and their principal officers, came to the ships soon after their taking over, and by January 25, 1918, two of the largest ships, *Roanoke* and *Housatonic,* were enough advanced to be commissioned. Living conditions were extremely rough amid the dirt and disorder, made worse by the slush and mud in the unpaved shipyards; but the presence of officers and men on board exerted constant forward pressure, while they were becoming acquainted with their ships. In the conversion of the *Shawmut* and *Aroostook* at Boston Navy Yard, the ships' companies worked in industrial gangs alongside the civilian employees, with such actual accomplishment and setting such an example, as to advance the date of completion materially. At the same time, their training progressed so well that, on June 16, 1918, only one week after completion, they started across.

Every 10 days or so during the five months shipyard work, I would go from Washington for a conference with the captains and the navy yard officers at New York and Boston, to keep in touch with the actual progress and the matters that appeared to need special attention. These conferences eliminated infinite writing and enabled closer touch to be kept with all preparations, additional effort to be more appropriately applied, than were possible by regular procedure alone, especially amid the swollen volume of correspondence in general. They developed, too, a good understanding among the officers, which made for future harmony and gained time towards the squadron's readiness.

Before the new ships were delivered, a special camp at Newport had been provided for training their crews under Mine Force officers. The *San Francisco* and *Baltimore* gave some practical instruction on board, and the camp was supplemented elsewhere, so that few, if any, wholly untrained men went to any ship. Three gun crews were trained in the battleships for each minelayer, and the engineer personnel were kept under training at Philadelphia until wanted. For the officers, similar measures were taken to put them in touch with the methods and experience of the Mine Force, as far as this could be done with ships most of the time at shipyards, fitting out.

Unlike the old Mine Force, the new was to consist of organizations on shore as well as afloat, and for this an officer of flag rank was wanted. Rear Admiral Joseph Strauss, U. S. N., was selected as the new Commander of the Mine Force.

Long identified with ordnance matters and of distinguished experience at the Naval Ordnance Proving Ground and Smokeless

Powder Factory, he was Chief of the Bureau of Ordnance for some years before going to command the U. S. Battleship *Nevada,* which he quitted to take command of the mine operation.   On February 15, 1918, he came to temporary duty in the Office of Naval Operations, where he familiarized himself with all information bearing on the operation and its preparation, and after a tour of inspection to the ships and acquainting himself with the mine situation, he sailed for England with his aid, Lieutenant Noel Davis, U. S. N.   On March 29, 1918, he assumed command of the Mine Force, with headquarters at U. S. Naval Base 18, Inverness, Scotland.   Thereupon the original Mine Force, consisting only of ships, became Mine Squadron One, and it became my part to complete its preparations in the United States and command the active force afloat.

The new Mine Squadron One was organized on Wednesday, April 10, 1918, at Hampton Roads, Virginia, on board the squadron flagship *San Francisco.*   I relieved Captain H. V. Butler, U. S. N., who had been in command of the Mine Force in the interval.   He remained as captain of the flagship and was also my chief-of-staff—the same association that we had in the old Mine Force.   Commander Bruce L. Canaga, U. S. N., who had been my invaluable assistant in Washington since the preparations began in November, came as my senior aid.

To us who had struggled through the long winter's difficulties, it was a memorable event when the first new minelayer, the *Roanoke,* Captain Stearns, joined the flag, on Friday, 12th April, 1918.   She was followed closely by the *Housatonic,* Commander Greenslade, and by the *Canandaigua,* Commander Reynolds, next day.   All was arranged for their loading with mines, and they began at once.   By a week later the *Quinnebaug,* Commander Mannix, and *Canonicus,* Commander Johnson, had joined, completing the number ready for service at that time.

Almost immediately the *Roanoke* was sent across ahead of the others, an inspection only 16 days after leaving the shipyard showing that her excellent condition warranted it.   She was to help the *Baltimore,* already there, to finish laying the minefield in the North Irish Channel, described in a previous chapter, but though she arrived in good season and ready, through a change of plan the *Roanoke* was not employed there, proceeding instead to Invergordon.

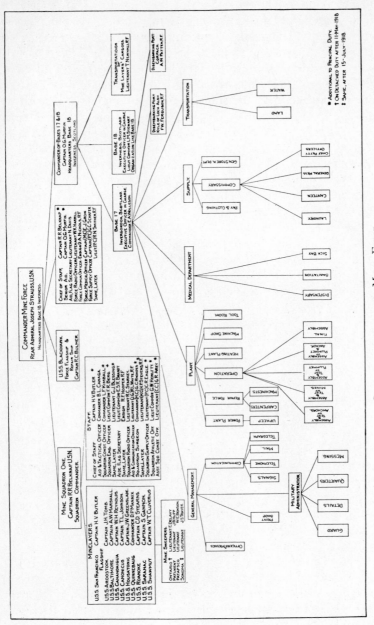

ORGANIZATION OF THE MINE FORCE.

The other four, with the *San Francisco,* continued the training program. An engine accident in the *Housatonic,* needing 10 days at Norfolk Navy Yard to repair it, delayed us a week, which was profitable for tying up the many loose ends left by the shipyards. Our second great event came on Sunday, 28 April, 1918, when the new squadron got underway together for the first time to exercise tactics and signals while en route from the Chesapeake for Provincetown. The day began and ended with steering gear troubles, and was followed by 40 hours of fog, which deprived us of valuable time that had been counted on. Tuesday, at 5 p. m., the *San Francisco* and *Housatonic* arrived at Provincetown. The *Canandaigua* was already maneuvering on the measured mile course while her diver was searching for a lost anchor. *Canonicus* was anchored inside. *Quinnebaug* reported herself anchored in the fog off Nantucket Lightship, repairing an engine break.

Next day, the morning fog lifted enough for all to begin standardizing over the measured course, afterwards proceeding to Gloucester Harbor, Massachusetts, where the final mine proving and the first practice minelaying by the new ships would be done. Strenuous days these, especially for captains! *Housatonic* asked permission to lag behind awhile, arriving at Gloucester very late. " Sorry to drag you over at this unchristian hour, Greenslade, but I wanted to see you about to-morrow's work." " Oh! never mind, sir. This is the *life!* "

Quinnebaug joined next afternoon, but she still needed some engine repairs which required navy yard assistance, and was accordingly ordered at once to Boston. More than unwelcome there with mines on board, the work and her departure were heartily speeded.

After scarcely any let-up since the ships had left the shipyards four weeks previously, a Sunday, May 5, 1918, was devoted to a well-earned rest. And now had to be decided whether to continue training longer or not. Outside of the ships singly, little had been done. They had not even been all together since the first evening at sea. Yet the mine bases were in such need of the 500 men that we were to bring them that, although only a meager part of the training had been carried out, it was decided to push on. There would be tactics and gunnery exercise en route, and possibly other training that had been omitted might be made up then too.

And so the original period of time, estimated as necessary to prepare, was adhered to, namely: in 45 days after leaving the shipyards to be at the North Sea base, with coal and mines on board, ready for a minelaying operation. Despite the numerous delays and mishaps, our arrival in Scotland, May 26, 1918, was on the fortieth day from the fifth ship leaving the yard, and all ships were ready for duty.

CHAPTER TWENTY-FOUR
AFTER THE WAR

The war over, the reorganized United States fleet was to include only the *San Francisco, Baltimore, Shawmut,* and *Aroostook* as minelayers. The Big Four ships were to bring troops home, and the *Quinnebaug* and *Saranac* to go back to their owners, the Old Dominion Steamship Company. The *San Francisco* needing repairs, the squadron flag was transferred temporarily to the *Baltimore.* This took place 17 January, 1919, at Newport, Rhode Island, whence we had sailed on our mission eight months before.

Never before in all my experience had I been in an organization where harmony, mutual confidence, good will, and loyalty prevailed so completely as in this Mine Squadron. The high spirit of the officers and men showed in the condition of their ships, their work, their discipline, and their individual personal bearing. To command such a body was an honor that could not be laid down in silence, and so, before the two pioneer minelayers parted, I spoke to their assembled officers and men as follows:

I am speaking to you to-day as representing the Squadron. It is very appropriate that, on this occasion of temporarily transferring the flag, I should get together the officers and crews of the two old war horses, *San Francisco* and *Baltimore,* that have made our success possible. The work in the Northern Mine Barrage did not begin only a year ago. It began for a squadron of mining ships when the *Baltimore* and the *Dubuque* joined the *San Francisco,* in the middle of 1915. These old ships set an example that made the rest aspire to follow, to live up to the high standard and steady pace necessary to accomplish what we have done.

To-day marks the end of the " Yankee Mining Squadron," that did four-fifths of the Northern Mine Barrage. I do not need to tell you how highly mentioned our work has been. When the reports have been published, no doubt it will be highly thought of in this country and by all who read about it in the future. This success is due, not to any one of us, not to any few of us, it is due to all of us. I am very proud to have commanded such a force. It is a deep gratification to have such a success come as a result of the efforts we have made through four years. Naturally, I shall never forget, but I wish to let you know that you should never forget it.

The Squadron is now reorganizing. Some of you may go to other duty, some may go out into civil life, where you will work during the conditions of peace which you helped to bring about. And now let me remind you of the principles on which we won success in our part in this war and on which we always did our work. Remember this! that the everyday things are the easiest to forget, and it is because we have carefully kept before us the importance of doing the everyday things right that we have earned success. We have not been afraid of work, we have never shied at any job. Every man has felt his part as important to do properly as any other man's part, and as long as the work was to be done he has kept up his attention. That has been the main principle—not to slack down—that a job is not finished until it is done, and it is not done until it is done right. We have not sought the easiest way but the right way, and we have generally found that the right way was the easiest way in the long run. And further, that a job, to be rightly done, must be as good at the end and in the middle as in the beginning. We have not slackened. The 860th mine of the *Canonicus,* of the longest string ever laid, was as good as the first or the 300th or any other mine.

I congratulate you all on the work you have done. It will be a very satisfactory and proud memory for you and for all those connected with it. But I congratulate you most on the preparation that it gives you to do still more, to be better men, to be better citizens. Nothing more valuable could come from our work than that.

You can fancy what my associations are with these two ships. I made my first cruise as a commissioned officer in the *Baltimore;* and the past four years in her and the *San Francisco* have been the most interesting I ever had. I am very sorry to leave you of the *San Francisco* even for a short time, but I could not leave under happier conditions. To leave at a time of a success like this happens only once in a lifetime. Good luck to all of you.

Long before the barrage was finished we were studying how to sweep it up, and soon after the signing of the armistice, experiment began towards safeguarding the sweeping vessels. Before leaving for home the squadron transferred over 400 men to the bases for the sweeping duty, and subsequently a number of new sweepers were sent over from the United States, in groups commanded by officers formerly of the mine squadron.

The British authorities took steps immediately to mark out the barrage area, with light-vessels and gas buoys, and actual sweeping began as early as December, 1918. It will take months to complete, but well inside a year from its laying the Northern Barrage will have become a thing of the past.

It served its purpose, and more besides. Through the part played in former wars, submarine mines grew in recognition, though slowly, as important means of defense. In this war they came into extensive employment in offense, the largest as well as most striking offensive use being the Northern Barrage, which, in popular phrase, put mines on the map.

SUMMARY OF MINES LAID

Excursions	1	2	3	4	5	5a	6	7	7a	8³	9⁴	10	11	12	13	Total
1. Canonicus	763	710	798	810	170	...	640	810	...	820	830	860	860	820	890	9781
2. Housatonic	769	800	840	830	320	...	...	810	...	820	830	860	840	820	800	9399
3. Canandaigua	775	710	760	779	170	...	640	810	...	820	830	840	840	855	...	8829
4. Roanoke	745	...	830	810	146	...	640	820	...	820	840	840	860	855	610	8206
5. Quinnebaug	...	...	600	600	...	...	610	590	...	600	600	610	610	615	610	6045
6. Saranac	...	...	597	580	...	...	...	...	...	560	600	610	610	615	610	4782
7. Aroostook	...	...	320	320	290	...	...	310	290	...	320	330	330	...	340	3180
8. Shawmut	...	...¹	300	320	150	...	330	320⁶	290⁵	270	320⁷	330	330	...	340	2970
9. San Francisco (Squadron Flagship)	153	...¹	170	170	170	166	160	170⁶	...⁵	170⁷	170⁶	170	170	170	170	2179
10. Baltimore	180	...	180	180	180	...	180	180	...	...	180	...	...	...	...	1260²
	3385	2220	5395	5399	1596	166	3200	4820	580	4880	5520	5450	5450	4750	3760	

Supplied by Base 17.....................28,930
Supplied by Base 18.....................27,641
          Total.....................56,571

Total distance steamed, from the assembly buoy and back...........8,383.5 miles
Total hours underway, from the assembly buoy and back............739 hours

Total U. S. Mines in Northern Barrage.. 56,571
Total laid by U. S. Squadron in the war. 57,470
British mines in Northern Barrage..... 13,546
Grand Total in Northern Barrage....... 70,117

¹ Present but not planting.   ² Plus 899 British mines laid in North Irish Channel.
³ Excursion by U. S. and British Minelaying Squadrons joined, Rear ⁴ Same, Rear Admiral Clinton-Baker, R. N., in command.
Admiral Strauss, U. S. N., in command.   ⁵ Flying the Squadron Commander's broad pennant for the excursion.
⁶ Flying the flag of the Commander of the Mine Force for the excursion.